P9-BZK-702

THE CHICAGO
HANDBOOK FOR
TEACHERS

THE CHICAGO HANDBOOK FOR TEACHERS:

ALAN BRINKLEY

BETTY DESSANTS

MICHAEL FLAMM

CYNTHIA FLEMING

CHARLES FORCEY

ERIC ROTHSCHILD

A PRACTICAL GUIDE TO THE COLLEGE CLASSROOM

THE UNIVERSITY OF CHICAGO PRESS / CHICAGO AND LONDON

Alan Brinkley is the Allan Nevins Professor of History at Columbia University. **Betty Dessants** is assistant professor of history at Florida State University. **Michael Flamm** is assistant professor of history at Ohio Wesleyan University. **Cynthia Fleming** is associate professor of cultural studies, history, and African-American studies at the University of Tennessee, Knoxville. **Charles Forcey** is a Ph.D. candidate in modern American intellectual history at Columbia University and vice president for new media at Clio Inc. **Eric Rothschild** is a history teacher who retired in 1998 as chair of the Social Studies Department at Scarsdale High School.

The University of Chicago Press, Chicago 60637
The University of Chicago Press, Ltd., London
© 1999 by The University of Chicago
All rights reserved. Published 1999
08 07 06 05 04 03 02 01 00 99   1 2 3 4 5
ISBN: 0-226-07511-7 (cloth)
ISBN: 0-226-07512-5 (paper)

Library of Congress Cataloging-in-Publication Data

The Chicago handbook for teachers : a practical
   guide to the college classroom / Alan Brinkley . . .
   [et al.].
      p.   cm.
   Includes bibliographical references (p.   ) and
index.
   ISBN 0-226-07511-7 (cloth : alk. paper). — ISBN
0-226-07512-5 (pbk. : alk. paper)
   1. College teaching Handbooks, manuals,
etc.   2. College teachers Handbooks, manuals,
etc.   I. Brinkley, Alan.
LB2331.C52332   1999
378.1'25—dc21   99-36617
                                                      CIP

CONTENTS

21.13/

97647

This book has a very simple purpose. It is designed to offer practical advice to teachers of college courses—advice on how to navigate many of the most common challenges they are likely to face in and out of the classroom. We expect it to be particularly helpful to beginning teachers, but we believe many experienced teachers will find the book useful and rewarding as well.

The project had its origins in a conversation about teaching at a meeting of the Executive Board of the Organization of American Historians several years ago, when two of the authors were members of the board. There was general agreement among the experienced scholars and teachers present that day that most beginning college instructors—graduate students having their first experiences as teaching assistants, new Ph.D.'s starting their first teaching jobs—received little or no training in how to deal with the classroom before they entered it. Primary and secondary school teachers ordinarily receive teacher training in education schools or departments. College and university teachers, by contrast, are usually trained intensively in their disciplines (history, English, economics, physics, and so on), but seldom in the craft of teaching itself. There is a growing, and heartening, movement in some graduate schools to incorporate teacher training into the traditional curriculum. But it remains the case that many, perhaps most, new college teachers design their courses and enter their classrooms for the first time without very much guidance from anyone. This book was written with them in mind. We call it a "handbook" because, while we think many teachers may wish to read it in its entirety, we believe others may wish to consult it periodically for help in dealing with particular questions or problems.

We do not claim here to present a coherent theory of teaching or learning. There are many such theories, and they are the subject of a large and valuable literature produced by scholars of education and others. Our goal, however, is the simpler one of answering common logistical questions and using our own experiences in the classroom to offer ideas and lessons that we think other teachers might find useful. In ten relatively brief chapters, we have tried to present practical suggestions for dealing with some of the basic aspects of college teaching: designing a course, preparing for the first class, leading a discussion, managing classroom dynamics, delivering a lecture, supervising research and writing, giving and grading exams, evaluating your own teaching, dealing with diversity issues, and making use of new electronic resources.

There are, needless to say, many issues related to teaching that this book does not address, and many ideas, techniques, and innovations for the classroom beyond those we have included. Both new and experienced teachers have many other resources from which they can draw as they try to improve their students', and their own, classroom experiences. We suggest some such resources in our brief bibliography, but there are also many others.

One problem that all teachers face to which we cannot offer any simple solutions is the problem of time. People outside the academic world often think of college or university teachers as people who live uniquely leisured lives. Those of us who actually work in academia know otherwise. Many of us enjoy more extended vacations than do people in most other professions, it is true. But during the teaching year, we are often compelled to balance an overwhelming number of commitments and responsibilities within a painfully short period of time: teaching classes, advising, grading, serving on committees, commuting, meeting obligations to families and communities, and so forth. Some teachers have very heavy course loads and can find very little time for each of the many preparations demanded of them. Other teachers have part-time jobs, sometimes several of them, and must scramble to find new work even as they are finishing the old. Many college teachers have to balance their teaching obligations against the pressure to do research and to publish, which are often prerequisites to professional survival.

No one will have time to implement all the suggestions in this book—let alone the many other ideas and suggestions available in other sources. Some people will have little time for any of them. We realize, therefore, that our prescriptions for teaching successfully will, in the world most teachers inhabit, need to be balanced against what is possible in pressured and difficult professional lives.

But teaching is a cumulative art. We learn over time, just as our students do. Things you have no time to try one year may be possible in another. A course that begins shakily may improve after two or three tries, and as you slowly incorporate new methods and techniques into your teaching. You should not be discouraged when the realities of your professional life make it hard to enhance your teaching quickly. Do what you can in the time you have, and over several years— if you keep working at it—your teaching will get better.

All of the authors of this book are historians, and our common experience in a single discipline has undoubtedly shaped the way we think about teaching. Teachers of English or psychology or chemistry or any other discipline would undoubtedly produce a rather different book. But almost everything we present here is, we believe, applicable to teaching in other fields—certainly to other disciplines in the humanities and social sciences, much of it also to the natural sciences and to the professional fields.

Teaching, particularly for the first time, can be a lonely and intimidating experience. We hope that the material we present here will make the experience less daunting and more rewarding—both for instructors and for their students.

We thank the many colleagues, friends, and family members who contributed, both directly and indirectly, to this book. Because there are six authors, the list of people who should be acknowledged is too long to include here, and we hope they will forgive us for not thanking them by name. We are also grateful to John Tryneski and the University of Chicago Press for their help in guiding this project to publication. Finally, we thank our students, who have taught us most of what we know about teaching—and many other things as well.

ONE

GETTING READY

Well before you first walk into the classroom, long before you meet your first student, you will make decisions about your teaching that will shape nearly everything that happens later. The first step in creating a successful course is planning and designing it, a task that usually begins months before the start of the term. It might begin with an early request from your library or bookstore for a list of your assigned readings. It might begin with a question from the registrar or some other administrator about what kind of classroom space you will need. It might begin with your department or your prospective students asking for copies of your syllabus. But whenever you make your first decisions, and whatever prompts you to make them, you and your students will have to live with them throughout your course. Thinking carefully in advance about how you structure your course, therefore, is the first step toward successful teaching.

Designing a course is difficult enough without trying to reinvent the wheel. There is no reason to be hesitant about borrowing ideas from others. Ask colleagues (in your own institution or in others) to share their materials from similar courses to get an idea of how others have taught the subject. Some departments maintain a file of syllabi for the use of both graduate students and faculty. Check the Internet, where an increasing number of academic departments and individual instructors have web pages with syllabi. Or contact appropriate professional organizations; they sometimes offer sample course outlines and syllabi.

However useful the ideas of others might be, you are the one who must teach the course you design. You must weigh any suggestions you receive against your own circumstances: the place of the course in your school's curriculum, the rules or expectations of your department, the nature of your students, and of course your own interests, commitments, and inclinations.

In planning a class, you need to think about three discrete yet integrated components of course design: (1) deciding what you want your students to learn, (2) choosing effective and appropriate course materials, and (3) creating a clear and informative syllabus.

WHAT DO YOU WANT YOUR STUDENTS TO LEARN?

This sounds like an obvious question, but it is one to which teachers do not always give sufficient thought. Part of the answer, of course, is embedded in the topic of the course. You expect your students to learn something about Shakespeare, or American government, or the Civil War, or whatever the subject of your course may be—although what they will learn about those subjects is something to which you must devote considerable thought. You must also think about what you want students to gain in conceptual knowledge and skills, and how you want them to gain it. Whether you are leading a large lecture class, a small research seminar, or something in between, the answers to these questions should help determine everything you do in your course.

One way to think about what you want your students to

learn is to begin conceptualizing your course from the end backward. You might construct questions that you would like your students to be able to answer on a final exam, or envision essay assignments that you would like your students to be able to tackle toward the end of the term. Once you have done that, begin thinking about what it will take to get your students to the point where they can do what you expect of them.

Getting students to that point requires considering carefully what material you wish to present to them: what you want them to read, what kind of research or other independent work you want them to do, what kind of problem sets you wish them to handle, what you want to discuss in class. You should think about the themes and skills you wish to emphasize in your course and what material will best serve them. The most stimulating book and the most engaging lecture will have little lasting impact on your students if it is not linked in some way to the larger purpose you want your course to serve. The thematic content of a course can be very simple or very complicated; it can be chronological or topical or theoretical or methodological. Whatever it is, it should be reasonably transparent, and the elements of the course should be designed to serve it. Do not, in other words, choose books or other material for your bookstore to order or your library to put on reserve and then decide later what themes you want to address in your course.

Thinking about how to get your students to achieve what you would like them to achieve also requires thinking about the way in which you want them to learn. Do you want students to learn to do serious research? If so, unless you have good reason to think your students have had significant research experiences before, you should organize your course so that research is an integral part of it from the beginning. You might, for example, assign a brief and relatively simple paper at the very beginning of the term to give students some early research experience and to give yourself a chance to evaluate their skills. Do you want your course to emphasize writing skills? If so, build in papers from the beginning and establish guidelines, both for your students and for yourself, about how the writing is to be evaluated and how improvement is to be measured. Do you want students to learn how to present ideas and arguments in public? If so, structure student presentations carefully and explain them clearly. Do you want your course to be a collaborative experience? If you do, decide at the start what role students are to play in the learning process and how they are to work together, and organize the course around those decisions.

You may not, of course, have complete freedom to design a course as you wish. In some cases, you may have very little freedom at all. If your course is part of a set curriculum, or if your syllabus is set by your department or by a committee, or if it is an introductory course designed as a gateway to other, more advanced courses, then you will have to plan your course to serve the objectives imposed on you. If you are a graduate student teaching a discussion section or conducting a lab, you will likely be serving a structure created by the supervising professor. Even then, however, you should give serious thought to how you wish to lead your students toward the course's goals, whether the goals are your own or those of others.

CHOOSING COURSE MATERIALS

Once you have given some thought to what you want your students to learn and how you want them to learn it, you can begin to think about what materials you can assign to them that will best serve your purposes. When choosing books and other materials, there are several things you should keep in mind.

First, think about the nature of your students and the

kind of preparation you can expect of them. At what level can they read? What skills are they likely to have? The material you choose should challenge your students, but it should not bewilder them. Many of the things that scholars find most interesting and exciting will be lost on students who do not have the preparation or skills to navigate through them.

Think also about the level of your students. If you are teaching an introductory course, your expectations—both for the amount of reading and for the difficulty of it—should be different from those for a course aimed at more advanced students. In a class of mixed levels, ask yourself whom you most want the course to serve and choose materials aimed at them.

Think carefully not just about the level, but also about the quantity of material you assign: how much reading and other work is it realistic to expect students to do? This too requires consideration of the nature and level of your students. It also requires you to think about the demands placed on them by other courses. If your students are taking five or six courses a term, your expectations for how much they can read for you will be lower than if they are taking three or four. Find out how much other teachers in your department expect. You may decide that your course should have a heavier or a lighter reading load than others, but you should at least be aware of what your students are accustomed to. Whatever you decide, try to assign roughly the same amount of work each week, with reductions periodically when papers or other projects are due, or when exams are scheduled. If you assign too much reading, your students simply will not do it all, and you will have little control over what they choose to read and what they do not.

You should think as well about the cost of the materials you are assigning. Given the escalating prices of textbooks, monographs, videos, and recordings, keep in mind the amount of money you are asking students to spend relative to how much they will use the materials in the course. If you ask students to purchase several books, be sure that you plan to make direct and specific use of them. You should, if possible, place everything you assign on reserve in your institution's library. (Find out how long the reserve process takes and allow sufficient time for the books to get there by your first day of class.) If your reserve system is a good one, and if your students are accustomed to using reserve readings, you can combine material you wish students to buy with material you place only on reserve. If your department has its own reading room, you might wish to create an informal reserve shelf of your own, with copies or photocopies of assigned reading available there. There is also an increasing amount of material available for free on the Internet, and you may wish to augment materials for purchase with web-based material—including, perhaps, material you yourself decide to place on a web site—if your students have ready access to the Internet.

USING VISUAL AND AUDIO MATERIALS

Books and other published materials are the traditional stuff of teaching, but there are many other resources available to you as well. As with assigned readings, you should think well in advance about what kinds of other materials—films, audio recordings, slides, overhead projections, computerized audiovisual material, class handouts—you wish to use.

Students usually respond well to visual and audio material—films, videotapes, and recordings—and the ready availability of such material in many forms makes their use much easier today than it was in the past. A videotape or a recording can be a diversion, with little relevance to the overall course goals. But if you prepare students for what they are going to see, and then engage them in a discussion or a writing exercise afterward, you can help ensure that visual and audio material will complement and not distract from written or spoken material.

Slides are more conventional visual aids and are, of course, integral to teaching in many fields, especially art history. But even if you are teaching a course that is not dependent on visual aids, slides can be a valuable complement to lectures and discussions. Check your institution's library and media centers for slide collections. Academic departments often have their own repositories, as do public libraries. You can also make your own slides (some institutions will do it for you). Again, choose your slides carefully, keeping in mind your goals for the particular lesson. And organize your slides well in advance of your classes, since it often takes time to locate or produce them.

Lectures and classroom discussions are often improved by the use of simple handouts in advance of or at the beginning of a class. Particularly effective are graphs, charts, data sheets, cartoons, photos, sketches, diagrams, and maps—many of which (depending on copyright laws) you can simply photocopy and distribute to your class.

Using transparencies with an overhead projector is an integral part of virtually all presentations—in both classrooms and professional meetings—in many disciplines. There are professionally prepared transparencies that might be useful to you, for example, the maps and charts that some textbook companies distribute to instructors. You can also make transparencies of your own, with presentation software such as Microsoft PowerPoint or simply by using a marker and writing directly onto the appropriate sheet. Preparing transparencies in advance can save you a great deal of time that you might otherwise spend in class writing on the blackboard. In large lecture halls, in particular, transparencies are often easier to see than material written on the board. As with slides, make sure your transparencies are carefully organized before you bring them to class.

As professors and students increasingly take advantage

of computer-based education, you may find prepackaged programs which allow you to supplement your lessons with multimedia presentations on CD-ROMs designed for laptops and screen projection. Ask at your school's media center or check publishers' catalogs to see if any might suit your needs.

Before you commit yourself to using visual, audio, or computerized materials, make sure that your institution can make the necessary facilities and equipment available to you and that you will know how to use them. It is both embarrassing to you and disruptive to your class to have to spend precious time fumbling with technology that does not work or that you do not know how to use. Also make sure that your classroom will be appropriate for the technologies you are using. If you plan to use slides or an overhead projector, for example, make sure your room has a screen, a table on which to place a projector, an electrical outlet appropriately located, and shades for windows. If you wish to use more sophisticated computerized materials, make sure that you have a room that is equipped for that.

FINDING COURSE MATERIALS

There are many resources that will help you identify and locate materials that might be useful for your teaching. If you are looking for ideas for books to assign, you might spend some time browsing through the catalogues of presses that publish prominently in your field. Once you have been teaching for a while, you will begin receiving such catalogues regularly in the mail. But it is an easy thing to request one from a publisher (using a toll-free number), and in many cases even easier to find catalogues and other information about new books at publishers' web sites. Browsing through bookstores—both the real things and the virtual stores such as Amazon.com and the Barnes and Noble web-based service—is another valuable way of discovering books you might wish to use. If you attend a large professional conference, publishers will likely be exhibiting their wares. Browsing through the book exhibits is a good way to get a sense of what new books are available; it is also often a good way to get free or discounted examination copies. Finally, informal discussion with fellow instructors about books that worked well—or didn't—can be very useful.

Once you have an idea of what books you might want to use, check for their availability in the current *Books in Print*— either in its printed form, available in libraries and bookstores, or on the Internet. The web-based booksellers are also convenient sources of information about what is in print, what is in paperback, and what things cost. They have the additional advantage of being places from which your students can order books if they are not available in the campus bookstore or if they are not discounted there.

Some books are published simultaneously in "trade" editions (which are sold in ordinary bookstores) and "college editions" (which are sold through the publisher's sales representatives and are ordered by instructors). Check to see which is less expensive. Publishers sometimes package texts with supplementary printed and audiovisual materials for students and instructors and sell them at reduced prices for the entire package. If you are ordering a textbook, check to see what materials are available to you and your students along with it and what you need to do to get them. Large college publishers ordinarily have sales representatives who visit campuses regularly. If you are interested in talking with one of them, contact the publisher in question and ask to have a sales representative contact you.

Be sure to get your order into your bookstore well enough in advance to ensure that the books are available when the course begins. Be sure as well to order "desk copies" for yourself and for your teaching assistants, if you have them. Many (but not all) publishers will send free copies of course books to instructors if they receive evidence that the

book has been adopted; if you can demonstrate a large enrollment, they will usually send multiple copies. They must be
ordered separately, using forms that are usually provided by
your campus bookstore or your department. Some publishers
have begun charging fees for desk copies and placing other
restrictions on them, so do not assume that all your requests
will be readily met. But there are still many publishers that
distribute free desk copies quite generously, and you should
take advantage of such opportunities when you can.

Most institutions and some academic departments maintain video, film, audio, and slide libraries for the use of faculty and students. If you wish to use any of your school's
material, find out what is available and how and when you
need to reserve it. Purchasing videos is often, but not always,
a more expensive proposition than buying books; local video
stores and mail-order companies sometimes sell documenta-
ries for less than twenty dollars. If there is a video series or
a CD collection that would be particularly useful for a widely
taught course, see if your department or library will purchase
it. *Bowker's Complete Video Directory* (three volumes), which
is updated every few years, is a useful guide to material on
videotape and is available in most libraries.

Internet-based scholarly networks sponsor electronic discussion groups or "lists" that often post user suggestions of
materials appropriate for all levels of courses in a variety of
disciplines. They also give you an opportunity to post questions to and solicit suggestions from professional colleagues
all over the country (or the world) about your teaching and
your research. In addition, many web sites contain material
that can be useful in the classroom.

PHOTOCOPIED PACKETS

Many instructors have solved the problem of tailoring assigned reading to their particular needs by making use of

packets of photocopied materials, which they then sell to their students. Photocopied packets can include excerpts from books; articles from journals, magazines, or newspapers; primary documents; or material created by the instructor. They become, in effect, the equivalent of a published reader, but one tailored to the precise needs of your course. Some instructors have such packets photocopied by their department or their university, which then makes them available to students for purchase. Others make use of professional photocopying stores, located near most campuses, which make the copies and sell them to students. A photocopied packet can be an excellent way to provide your students with exactly the readings you want to assign them.

But it also has serious drawbacks, mostly connected with the copyright laws protecting the original sources. Almost anything published within the last seventy-five years by a commercial or scholarly press is covered by copyright, and it is illegal to sell or distribute copies without receiving permission from the copyright holder and, usually, paying a fee. (Most government documents are not copyrighted and can be copied and distributed at will.) If you are creating an elaborate packet with many different elements, it will be time consuming and expensive for you to contact all the publishers yourself and arrange the appropriate permissions. And yet without permissions, you cannot realistically continue with the packet. Commercial photocopiers (some of whom have been the subject of costly lawsuits by publishers over this issue in recent years) will now usually refuse to copy material without the appropriate letters of permission. Your department and university will likely have the same requirements. Many instructors have simply given up on photocopied packets in face of these seemingly overwhelming difficulties.

There are, however, alternatives to acquiring the permissions yourself or giving up. Commercial photocopiers such as Kinko's sometimes offer a service whereby they obtain all permissions for you and add the cost of them to the packet before selling it to students. This will save you a great deal of time and aggravation, but it might also add significantly to the cost of the packet and make it unaffordable for your students. Be sure to get an estimate of the final cost before proceeding. Obviously the smaller the packet, or the fewer copyrighted items in it, the lower the cost will be.

Articles in many scholarly journals published more than five years ago are now available for free on the Internet through an extraordinary web site—www.jstor.org—if your university is a participating member. Try accessing the site through your institution's web site to see if you and your students are eligible to use it; if not, check with the information technology officer at your institution to see if membership is an option. If you can obtain access to JSTOR, you can assign any article that has appeared in dozens of leading journals (except those that have appeared in the last five years) simply by referring students to the web site. That may significantly reduce the size and cost (especially since journals often charge high permission fees) of your photocopied packet or eliminate the need for one altogether.

Some educational publishers, and even a few universities, now provide custom publishing services through which you can assemble a reader that will be custom printed for your class from a list of materials they provide. Some such providers will add materials to their data bank at your request. This is usually cheaper than paying copyright fees through a photocopy service, but the expense can still be significant. You also usually have a smaller range of choices than you would have if you were assembling material on your own. Nevertheless, some instructors have found these custom publishing services to be of great value.

Copyright issues, both for printed and web-based materials, are a constant challenge to instructors trying to find a way to assign the material they want without relying on overburdened library reserve systems and without requiring their students to spend too much money. It will take some time and ingenuity on your part to make published materials available within the copyright laws. But if you want to teach with assignments of your own devising, you may find that it is worth it to make the effort.

PREPARING A SYLLABUS

The syllabus is the central document of your course. It introduces students to your expectations, guides them through assignments, and provides them with a schedule and other important information. If your syllabus is well organized and informative, it can be of enormous value in getting your course properly started and in keeping students on track through the term. The process of preparing a syllabus can also be of great value to you, in forcing you to think through the structure and organization of the course, in helping you make decisions about what and how much material you can realistically expect to cover in the short time you have, and in working out how you can best organize that material.

A good first step in preparing a syllabus is to make, in effect, a calendar of the term. Prepare a list or chart of the weeks, or class days, that your institution's academic calendar makes available to you—and of the specific days on which your class will meet. Take account of holidays and other breaks in the schedule. Then begin scheduling lectures, classes, reading and paper assignments, and exams accordingly.

As you schedule your assignments, be sensitive to the time pressure students face both in your own course and in others. Don't make a paper due a few days before or after an exam, or the Monday after a homecoming weekend, or the day before Thanksgiving. Don't schedule your heaviest reading assignments for midterm week. Keep in mind that many courses assign papers that are due at the end of the term, and consider whether you can schedule yours earlier to avoid getting caught in the crunch.

Once you have scheduled your classes and assignments, you should consider the format and contents of the syllabus itself, keeping in mind that for many students it is their first introduction to your course. Make sure it is informative, thorough, and—not unimportant—visually clear, neat, and attractive.

The top of the first page of any syllabus should present certain basic information: the name of your institution, the semester and year, the course's full title, number, and (when relevant) the number of credits it represents. It should also include your own name, your office address, and (depending on your preferences) your telephone number and/or e-mail address. If you know what your office hours will be well enough in advance of the term, you should include those as well.

The syllabus should then provide a brief description of the objectives and procedures of the course. You might include a paragraph or two laying out the central themes, questions, or skills that the course will emphasize. You should certainly explain how the course is structured (how often it will meet, what the format of the meetings will be) and what your expectations are. You should state clearly what the assignments will be (papers, readings, discussions, labs, exams, etc.) and how much you plan to weight each element in calculating a grade. Students should know whether attendance will be taken and whether class participation is to be included as part of the grade. They should know when papers are due, where they should be handed in, what the procedures are for getting extensions, and what the penalties are for lateness. They should know the dates of exams and the procedures for rescheduling or taking makeups. You may not wish to include all this material on the syllabus itself, particularly if some of these issues are complicated and will take considerable explanation. But the more basic information you place on the syllabus, the less class time you will need to spend explaining rules and procedures.

Among the services a syllabus performs for your students is to give them a clear guide to what books they need to buy or borrow at the beginning of the term. To make that task easier, you should consider providing a simple list of all the reading or other assignments near the beginning of the syllabus, in roughly the order in which you have assigned them—even if you are going to repeat the information later in the course schedule. Students should not have to thumb through a complicated schedule in order to know what books to pick up in the bookstore.

The most important part of the syllabus is usually the weekly or daily schedule of topics and assignments. If you are giving a lecture course, you might list the subjects or titles of your lectures along with the reading assignments that accompany them. If you are teaching a seminar or a discussion course, make clear what material is to be discussed in each class. Even if you have stated due dates for papers and dates for exams at the top of the syllabus, include them again in your schedule. Identify holidays as well. Students should be able to rely on your schedule for planning their work in the course, and the fuller it is the more useful it will be to them.

Some institutions require that every syllabus in every course contain certain information, such as procedures for students with disabilities, a statement of academic honesty, or the final exam schedule. Make sure you are aware of any such mandated information before you complete your syllabus.

You will dramatically reduce the potential for misunderstandings if you are explicit about your goals, expectations, and requirements on the syllabus. Once you have typed it, review it for readability, format, completeness, and accuracy. Proofread carefully for errors, match days of the week with corresponding days of the month (few things are more confusing to students than calendar errors), and review institutional requirements. Then ask yourself about the tone of your syllabus. If you were a student reading this syllabus for the first time, what impression would you have of the course and of the teacher? Are you conveying enthusiasm for the subject? Is your syllabus a fair representation of the course you will teach? The syllabus should give an accurate impression of both you and the course it describes.

Finally, you need to be aware of the limits of your preparation. Despite the most careful planning and preparation, no course will follow your expectations exactly. As important as it is to prepare carefully in advance, it is also important, from the first day of class, to be attentive to your students' reactions and performances and to be flexible enough to make changes when you think they may be helpful to your class or when things are going wrong.

TWO
THE FIRST
WEEKS

The first few weeks of the term may well be the most difficult for you, particularly if you are a new teacher. But they are also the weeks in which the character of a course is established. If your students are not drawn into the material you wish them to learn at the beginning, if the classroom dynamic is not a comfortable one at the start, it may be difficult to improve things as you move along.

PREPARING FOR THE
FIRST CLASS

The first day of class can be the most important day of the term. Especially if you are new to the classroom, it is also the day when you will probably be the most nervous. It might help to remember that your students may be even more nervous than you are, and that even experienced teachers usually approach the beginning of a course with some anxiety. (Just as students often have anxiety dreams about walking unprepared into an exam, so many teachers have similar dreams before a term begins about walking unprepared into a lecture or class.)

In preparing for your first class, you should think about several things. You should, of course, prepare intellectually; you need to know the material you will be asking your students to learn. Equally important, especially if you are a new teacher, is deciding on a style and tone that will be effective in the classroom. The first rule of thumb is to choose a classroom style that is comfortable for you. Do not try to make your classroom persona wholly different from your normal self. Students will usually recognize an artificial posture sooner or later, and you will probably be unable to sustain an unnatural teaching style for very long in any case. But that does not mean that you should behave in the classroom exactly as you would behave in other places. Your instincts may tell you to be casual and informal; but you also need to convey to your students that you take them and the project you are beginning with them seriously, and that they should do the same. If you begin a class with at least a small amount of formality, it is relatively easy to move from there to a friendlier and more casual tone as you move along. It is much more difficult to reverse the process.

Think carefully about how you wish to present yourself in the classroom. What you wear, how you address your students (first names, last names), how you ask them to address you, whether you stand or sit or pace—all of these things help establish your style and identity in the students' minds. Consider what kind of relationship you wish to establish with your students, and behave in ways that are consistent with that. Decide in advance how you wish to communicate with your students outside the classroom. Do you wish to give students your phone number—and do you want them to call you at home? Do you want to encourage them to communicate with you by e-mail? Establish the ground rules of your relationship with them early to avoid misunderstandings later.

The physical arrangement of your classroom can make a difference too. In many cases, you may have no control over how a classroom is arranged. But if you do, think about the configuration with which you will feel most comfortable. How students sit on their first day in class, and where you position yourself in relation to them, can contribute to the impression they have of the dynamics of a course. If you are teaching in a room with movable desks or chairs, decide whether you want students to sit in a circle, as if around a seminar table, to facilitate discussion; or in rows facing forward, to facilitate lectures and presentations. Visit the room in advance and think about what possibilities, and problems, it presents.

How do you want to arrive in class? Arriving early and talking with students as they walk in may help you, and them, to relax. Arriving at just the moment the class is scheduled to begin may help you avoid possible awkwardness in switching from casual conversation to the more structured dynamics of the actual class. Arriving late is not an acceptable option, particularly if you want (as you should) to establish an expectation among your students that they should be on time.

DECIDING WHAT TO TEACH ON THE FIRST DAY OF CLASS

The best way to know how to start any class is to know what you want your students eventually to achieve. That is no less true on the first day than on any other. Give them a clear sense at the beginning of what you expect of them in your course, and what you want them to expect of themselves. Make clear what your requirements will be. Establish whatever rules you think are appropriate. But also use your first class to give students at least a preliminary taste of the substance of your course. Some teachers simply start at the beginning, and make few concessions to the fact that students are there for the first time. They say, in effect, we are here to do something important, and we are going to start doing it without delay. Other teachers use the first class to offer a particularly engaging sample of what they want their students to learn. They might assign an exercise that will give students the experience of mastering a technique or a small body of knowledge right away. They might present a lecture that tells a particularly vivid or captivating story that will capture students' interest early in the course. They might distribute a document or problem set and invite students to respond to it, giving them a hands-on experience of interpretation or analysis or methodology at the very beginning. Whatever you do, pick something you care about and can teach with energy.

The first class, naturally, is also the time to distribute your syllabus and to explain procedural matters. If you have prepared your syllabus well, you should not have to spend too much time discussing the mechanics of the course. But be sure to devote at least some time to establishing procedures and answering students' questions. If you expect the procedural discussion to be brief, you might wish to get it out of the way at the very beginning of class. If you expect it to be long and complicated, you might save it for the last part of the class and use your first minutes with your students to deal with something more interesting and challenging.

In some institutions students are encouraged to "shop" for courses before selecting them. Because many students may be deciding whether or not they wish to take your course, give them an experience on the first day that will show them what you think is best about it—but also one that will give them a sense of what is expected of them. Students who are unwilling to participate in a class discussion, for example, should learn immediately that your class is not appropriate for them if you value participation. Some students may miss your first day's class because they are observing other teachers, and some students who come the first day may not return. So don't organize your course so rigidly that a change in enrollment will derail your plans.

One of the most important things you can do on the first day of a class in which discussion and participation are at the heart of the effort is to engage your students right away. Find a way to get everyone to say at least something. Try to elicit thoughts from students who seem reluctant to talk. Establish at the beginning that this is a shared enterprise, that students are expected to be active participants in your joint project, not passive observers.

MAKING INTRODUCTIONS

In a very large class, it may be unrealistic to ask students to introduce themselves to each other and to you. Even in a smaller class, the chaos of the first day—especially in a school where students may not yet be committed to the course—can be a difficult time for introductions. But somewhere near the beginning of any course small enough to make it possible for you to know your students, you should consider spending some time having them introduce themselves.

There are many ways to do this. The simplest is just to ask students to tell the class who they are. But the simplest approach often produces the simplest, and least useful, results. If fifteen or twenty students simply state their names one after the other, neither you nor they are likely to learn or remember very much from the experience. More productive is encouraging students to say something of substance about themselves—to say where they are from, what interests or activities they are involved in outside of class, what their major or their area of concentration is, if they have one. Some instructors ask students to think of one interesting fact about themselves and present it to the class. Others ask students to introduce not themselves, but the person sitting next to them; each student "interviews" the other and then presents the results.

Of course, you should introduce yourself as well. But since you are older and more experienced, you may have a great deal more to tell about yourself than they do. Keep your own introduction relatively short so as not to create an impossible standard for your students when they present theirs, but say enough to give them a sense of what an appropriate introduction should be. You can also introduce yourself after the students are done.

ESTABLISHING THE
DYNAMICS OF A CLASSROOM

Many good teachers try to establish from the beginning that they expect their students to be active participants in the classroom—that the purpose of the course is not teaching, but learning. That usually means requiring students to take some responsibility for the conduct of the course and to take some risks in the process of learning. Since many students may find such expectations new and unusual, you need to work carefully to help them meet them. Much of your success in doing so will depend on how you establish the dynamics of your classroom in the first week or so of the term. If you are teaching a large course in which you have limited personal contact with your students, the task of motivating them comes from how you present yourself to them and what you ask them to do on their own. But in smaller courses, where it is possible to know your students, there are many more opportunities—and sometimes many more problems.

In defining the dynamics of your class, you should first think carefully about how close you wish to become to your students. If you are too much a "friend," you may diminish your effectiveness in inspiring or motivating them.

You might also find yourself tempted to begin inappropriate relationships with your students if you develop too personal a relationship with them. In today's academic world, with its heightened sensitivity about sexual harassment, personal relationships between instructors and students require great care. An accusation of sexual harassment can destroy a professional career irrevocably—not to mention the damage an inappropriate relationship can do to a student. Instructors should never forget, therefore, that the position of authority in which they find themselves in relation to their students makes sexual relationships, or even nonsexual but otherwise intimate personal relationships, inadmissible in the academic world. Most instructors would not consider initiating or entering such a relationship, but even they should be careful to do nothing that might be misunderstood. Do not put yourself in a situation where an effort to be friendly might be misinterpreted as an effort to establish an inappropriate relationship.

On the other hand, avoiding an inappropriate relationship does not mean having no relationship with students. It is perfectly appropriate, often even desirable, to have friendly relationships with students, to meet with them outside of class, even to have social interaction with them. You might take students for lunch or for coffee—preferably in groups, and preferably in settings that are appropriate for that purpose. You might invite them to your home for dinner—again, especially if you are single, usually in groups, not individually. It is probably not a good idea for an instructor, even a graduate instructor, to attend undergraduate parties at which his or her students may be present, or to take students out drinking.

Whatever you decide, you should, if possible, know who your students are. Learn their names. Some teachers use a "face book" before a class meets to learn and memorize names, but most teachers have no such option. Careful introductions at the beginning can help. So can asking students to state their names briefly at the beginning of subsequent classes to allow them to remind you and each other of who they are. (Make sure to ask all students, even those you know, to introduce—or reintroduce—themselves, to avoid revealing which names you have not learned.) You might also ask them to identify themselves when making a comment in class during the first few meetings, and ask them to sit in the same seats each week until you learn their names. If you are not good at remembering names, tell them that and make clear that you will be making a real effort to overcome the problem. Or ask students to place their names on small signs in front of them, and explain to them that this is to help you learn their names and also to help them get to know one another. Nothing is more dispiriting to students in a small class than a sense that the instructor does not know who they are. Worst of all is when a teacher learns some names and not others; those whose names the teacher does not learn can easily come to feel anonymous and marginal.

Find out what you can about your students—their majors, their particular interests, their backgrounds. Introductions at the beginning of the term are one way to do this, as noted above. You might also ask students to fill out note cards giving you their names, contact information, and some pertinent facts about themselves, so that you will have a record to which you can refer. If you know something about your students, you can target your questions more effectively and often give reticent students a chance to participate more comfortably.

Help your students to know each other. The more students get to know one another, the more comfortable they will feel interacting with one another—both in and out of class. Here again, introductions—the more informative the better—can help. It also helps to distribute a list of everyone in the class early in the term, with names, addresses, phone numbers, e-mail addresses, and so forth (although you should be sure to ask students for permission before you distribute any information about them to others). Getting students involved early in the term in projects or assignments that require collaboration is another good way to help them feel comfortable with and connected to one another.

Perhaps most important, treat your students with respect. Do not belittle them. Do not embarrass them in front of their peers. Do not confuse browbeating and intimidating with motivating. There was a time when it was common in higher education for larger-than-life teachers to tyrannize students and intimidate them into working harder. But in today's academic culture, such tactics will usually seem bizarre and alienating. It is perfectly appropriate to be critical of students' work, to point out mistakes. But it is possible to do so without being contemptuous, abusive, or disrespectful.

DEALING WITH PASSIVE, VOLUBLE, OR DISRUPTIVE STUDENTS

You will probably have no control over who enrolls in your class. But you do have choices to make about how to deal with them once they are there. Those choices are particularly important if you find, as teachers often do, that there are problem students in the class. It is very important, therefore, to establish your ground rules early—and particularly your ground rules for dealing with students who are passive, excessively voluble, or openly disruptive.

Most classes include students who participate actively and others who remain passive. In dealing with passive students, it is important first to try to understand why they are silent. In some cases, you may find otherwise voluble students remaining quiet because they have taken some dislike to the class or to you. If you sense that is the case, you might try to have a conversation with the students in question to try to find out what the problem is. Unchecked, alienation of that sort can infect others. More often, however, passive students are quiet because they are intimidated by you or the class, or have convinced themselves—or been convinced by others—that they have nothing interesting to say.

There may be students who are so shy or so insecure that no amount of prompting will draw them effectively into the dynamic of the classroom. But you should nevertheless make a serious effort to engage all your students, and you should begin those efforts at the very beginning of the term so that your expectations are clear and so that students can begin to feel comfortable speaking in the group from the start. In dealing with passive students in your first weeks, there are several tactics you can use. The simplest and most obvious is to call on quiet students rather than waiting for them to volunteer. You might arrange to meet with such students individually outside class, explain the importance of participation, and try to prepare them for the next discussion. You might share with the student in advance a question that you plan to raise in the next class. Or you might ask students to work together in small groups—either before or during part of a class—to prepare a presentation or an argument. Some students who seem unusually reticent in the structured setting of a class discussion are much more relaxed in small, less formal groups.

Excessively talkative students can present an equally serious problem. If a student dominates a class so thoroughly that other students are unable to participate adequately, you need to act. One way to do so is to talk with garrulous students outside class: assure them that you value their comments, but make clear to them that they must restrain themselves and make space for other students to participate. In the classroom itself, you can prevent a single student from dominating the class by taking charge of the discussion so that you are the one who chooses who is to speak, as opposed to allowing the conversation to flow spontaneously.

A more difficult problem is a student who may or may

not speak often, but who speaks at excessive length when called on. Longwinded students require some patience, but at some point it is necessary to intervene if a comment goes on so long that it threatens to deflate a discussion. Such an intervention is particularly important if the student is confused and unclear, as is often the case, and continues to speak because he or she cannot figure out how to bring comments to a conclusion. It is always difficult to interrupt or cut off students, and teachers are usually (and appropriately) reluctant to embarrass them by doing so. But in some cases, an interruption is essential to the dynamic of the class as a whole. Often, it will actually be a relief to the student in question.

There are sometimes students who, intentionally or inadvertently, become disruptive. It can be a relatively passive disruption—for example, students who read or work on other material while you are teaching. It is perfectly appropriate to ask such students to stop. It is also sometimes helpful, if you wish to avoid a direct confrontation, to wait until the beginning of the next class and simply announce to everyone that it is not acceptable for students to read or do other work while you are teaching. You may also encounter active disruption. Students may get in the habit of coming late or leaving early; make clear to them—and to everyone—that you expect them to come and go on schedule. (Some students have legitimate reasons to come late or leave early on certain days, in which case you should insist that they notify you in advance; and you might consider explaining to the rest of the class why one student is violating the schedule to make clear that they should not do the same.)

Some students may say antagonistic or explosive things to see how you will react. If the comment, whatever its intent, is worthy of a serious response, then take it seriously—and ask other students to respond to it. But if the disruption takes the form of language or comments that are simply offensive, a different kind of response is necessary. Some kinds of comments are intolerable in class and must be challenged, even rebuked. You should make clear to your class, if such problems arise, that you will not tolerate certain kinds of remarks in class (for example, comments disparaging a person's race, gender, appearance, or sexual preference), and you should react even more forcefully if they are directed at other members of the class. It is, of course, often difficult to decide when a comment crosses the line between being a legitimate part of intellectual discussion and being gratuitously offensive speech; in an academic setting, the threshold for unacceptable ideas and language should be very high. In most cases, the best way to deal with difficult or offensive speech in class is to permit other students to respond to it and challenge it. But teachers have responsibilities to themselves, and to their students, to keep their classrooms open and tolerant places. As difficult as it may be to decide when to intervene, you should be prepared to do so—and to do so forcefully—when you feel certain that students are speaking inappropriately and offensively in ways that threaten the atmosphere of trust that is essential in any class.

ESTABLISHING THE
DYNAMICS OF OFFICE HOURS

Some instructors may have many opportunities to meet with students outside of class. For most, however, the usual occasion other than class time for meeting students is office hours. Just as it is important to establish the dynamic of your classroom early, you should also establish the character of your office hours from the start.

The most important thing for you to do during your office hours is to be there. Office hours are not a casual commitment; nothing is more likely to frustrate and anger your students than for them to come to your office at the appointed time and not find you. During office hours, leave your door open. Some students may interpret a closed door as a signal that you are busy.

Schedule your office hours at times likely to be convenient for your students. Early Monday morning and late Friday afternoon are bad times. Immediately before or after class is often a good time. If there are students who are consistently unable to make your office hours because of other commitments, try to find other times to talk with them. Encourage students who have trouble matching their schedules with yours to use e-mail, which can, in effect, extend your office hours and make them accessible to busy students. It surely makes it more difficult for students to claim that you are not available.

If you have your own office, by all means use it. But if necessary establish an appropriate place—a professor's vacant office, an empty classroom, a place in the library where talking is permitted, if necessary a table in a coffee shop or cafeteria (ideally a quiet one)—where you can conduct meetings regularly. Avoid using your home, or any other nonpublic place. Students may feel uncomfortable and even misinterpret your motives.

Your best intentions, the most appealing office, and the ideal time will not matter at all if students fail to come. Getting students to visit you during office hours requires some effort on your part. That begins with active encouragement in class—making clear that you are not only available but eager to see students. It can also help to establish requirements. Early in the course, you might require each student to schedule a meeting with you to discuss an upcoming paper or assignment or a particularly difficult reading—or simply to discuss the course and their early reactions to it. (Requiring such meetings has the additional advantage of giving you a structured opportunity to talk with students who are having, or causing, problems without singling them out.) After students have come to see you once, even if involuntarily, the prospect of coming again will seem less intimidating. In larger classes, in particular, you might consider group sessions, in which you encourage (or require) several students to come to your office together for an appointment.

When a student arrives in your office, put down any other work you are doing immediately. Don't answer the phone while the student is there, or if you must, keep your conversation brief. (Some instructors establish a limit to the number of interruptions they will allow during a student's visit; they might, for example, answer the first telephone call and ignore later ones.) Most important, try to determine why the student has come to you. Often, this will be obvious. Students will have questions about assignments, will want extensions on papers, or will have specific questions about material you've covered in class. Sometimes, however, students will come to office hours simply to meet you but will not be certain what to do once they have done that. You can help by asking them to tell you something about themselves and otherwise suggesting that you are pleased to see them and interested in talking with them. At other times, students will have problems—intellectual or personal—that they want to discuss with you but are afraid to bring up. Again, it is important for you to show an interest in them and not express impatience when they are not immediately clear about what they want.

Although you should never dismiss a legitimate concern or question from a student, you should not agree to inappropriate requests either. Students who have missed many classes and assignments and want you to "fill them in" are not making reasonable requests. You should tell them what they can do to catch up, but you should make clear that catching up is their responsibility, not yours.

Do not attempt to take on burdens beyond your expertise or experience. You should listen respectfully and sympathetically to personal problems and help if you think you can. But there are many problems that you will be unequipped to handle. Be familiar with the support services of your institution so that you can, if necessary, refer a student to a trained professional. Remember that you can sometimes do more harm than good if you try to help a student with a serious problem that you do not fully understand. If you sense that a student is in truly serious difficulty, you should notify the appropriate dean or other official immediately to ensure that someone monitors the situation.

Sometimes individual students may try to monopolize your time—because they like you, because they think spending time with you will benefit them in some way, or because they are naturally longwinded. It is important to find a gracious way of limiting the time one student can spend with you, especially when there are other students waiting or you have appointments pending. Keeping the door open during office hours so that your visitors can see whether other students are waiting can help here. Doing so may discourage a single student from staying too long. But if necessary, it is perfectly appropriate, after a reasonable period, to tell a student that you must now speak with the next person in line. Or you can begin each session with a statement that you cannot speak indefinitely because other students are waiting or are expected.

There are no sure things in teaching. No matter how talented, how well prepared, and how hard working you are, some classes—and some entire courses—will not live up to your expectations. Many things are outside your control. But if you organize a course carefully, begin a class effectively, and prepare your students fully for what you expect of them; if you establish a cordial, even lively atmosphere in your classroom; if you convince your students that you are interested in them and their work; then your chances of success will greatly improve.

THREE

CLASSROOM
DISCUSSIONS

The ability to lead a good discussion is the heart of effective teaching. Discussions of various kinds are the most common form of teaching at almost all levels, and for many students and teachers the most challenging and rewarding. A successful discussion is an exciting, even a memorable, experience for everyone involved, and one of the great joys of teaching.

But leading a discussion is one of the most difficult and unpredictable of all teaching experiences. Most teachers know the feeling of coming to the end of a class excited and eager for more. But virtually all teachers also know the feeling of trying to create a good discussion and failing. Some things may be partially or wholly outside your control: the talents, preparation, or mood of your students; problems in getting access to necessary material; distracting outside events; even the weather or the flu. Many teachers have had the experience of doing the same things with the same material in two different classrooms and having entirely different results. Sometimes discussions fail—or at least fail to sparkle—no matter what you do, so you should keep their unpredictability always in mind. But there are techniques by which you can make failure much less likely.

VARIETIES OF CLASSROOM
DISCUSSION

Classroom discussions take many different forms, from large lecture courses in which instructors elicit student participation (see chapter 4) to very small seminars or even tutorials in which the discussion becomes something close to a personal conversation.

Despite the differences among various forms of discussion, some things are common to almost all of them. The quality of the discussion itself is always important, as is the willingness and ability of all students to participate in it; discussions are critical to learning because they make students active participants in the process. But discussions are not simply occasions for interesting conversations or for students to have opportunities to talk. They are also occasions for students to learn—to receive information, to consider arguments, to develop skills, or to test ideas. However student-centered the discussion may be, the instructor must be alert to its character and ready to intervene to ensure that it remains productive. A discussion can fail if students feel barred from participating. It can also fail if, at the end, students feel they have not learned anything from it.

The most common kinds of discussion fall into two categories. One common method of leading a discussion is for the instructor to orchestrate the conversation through Socratic methods: asking questions, responding to the answers, and asking more questions, trying to lead the class in the direction the teacher has previously decided it should go. Perhaps the most famous example of the Socratic discussion in modern education is the law school classroom dialogue between students and professor, which—at least as presented in film and on television—is often a tense, even confrontational fencing match. In other settings, however, such discussions are usually much less formal and much less confrontational. They can be a good way for a teacher to combine traditional "instruction," presenting information to students that the teacher believes they need, with student participation. Such discussions often take place in traditional classrooms, with the instructor in the front of the room and the students facing him or her from desks or tables arranged in rows or semicircles; but they can, of course, take place in any setting.

A very different kind of discussion, generally associated with the concept of the seminar, is one in which the teacher tries to serve mainly as a mediator and guide to a conversation among the students themselves. A seminar instructor usually asks questions of the students, at least at the beginning of class, but less to elicit particular answers and lead the class along a rigidly predetermined path than to stimulate conversation and debate among the students. These discussions often occur around a seminar table, with the instructor usually seated either at the head of the table, if it is rectangular, or randomly among the students, if the table is round or square. If there is no table, and the chairs or desks in the classroom are movable, a teacher can prepare for a seminar discussion by having students arrange their seats in a circle. It is difficult to run a seminar in a conventional classroom with fixed desks all facing forward, but it is not impossible—and of course there may be times when that is the only space available.

A Socratic discussion can take place in a class of almost any size, although the larger the class, the more inhibited students are likely to be about speaking up. (The famous law school Socratic dialogues often involve hundreds of students, but in those classes the professor usually selects people to question at random from a class list; that technique is much more difficult in most undergraduate courses, with their more heterogeneous populations.) A seminar discussion is difficult to sustain in a group of more than twenty students, and works best with a group of eight to fifteen.

PREPARING FOR A
DISCUSSION

Preparation is at least as critical to a successful discussion as it is to a successful lecture. Indeed, some instructors use lecture-like outlines in preparing for a class discussion (although those who do so often have great difficulty steering their class along the route they have prepared). Most teachers prepare in a less rigidly structured way. But however you prepare, there are certain basic steps you should take in getting ready for your class.

First, you should, naturally, be familiar with the material your students are gathering to discuss and be ready to answer questions about it and to place it in its proper context. Second, as in any class, you should have goals for your discussion: issues you want your students to consider, questions you want them to answer, problems you want them to encounter. You may, and probably should, be reasonably flexible about how they reach the goals you have set and whether they reach all of them, but you should be ready to ensure that, one way or another, they do reach some of them. If, as is often the case, the points you wish the discussion to address build on one another, you should have a rough idea of the sequence you want the class to follow—the question with which you want them to begin, and the order in which you want them to move through the material. You may find that you do not need to follow the plan you have made, that the discussion moves in directions you do not anticipate but nevertheless welcome. But it is always a good idea to have a plan of your own, in case you find you need it.

Students need to prepare for discussions just as much as the instructor, and in a course that depends on participation you need to make clear at the start that everyone should be ready and willing to play an active role in class. Usually, such preparation will mean doing assigned reading or other exercises; and thus much of the task of ensuring adequate preparation rests on encouraging students to complete these assignments before they come to class. Giving your students some insight into the assignments in advance—either by talking about them in an earlier class or distributing questions and guidelines for readings or exercises before the discussion—can help lead them into material that some might otherwise find obscure. But if encouragement and exhortation are not enough, you can try some slightly more coercive tactics: assigning a short paper on the topic ahead of time that will require them to think about the material you will be discussing; or giving a brief in-class writing assignment on the reading at the start of the class period.

A different way of motivating students to prepare for class is to make a regular habit of calling on all members of the group, even letting students know that you intend to grade them in some way on their participation. But the best way to motivate students, of course, is to help them become excited about the subject, the class, the assignments, and even about you.

STARTING A DISCUSSION

Beginning a discussion is often difficult, particularly early in the term, when the students do not yet know one another, or you, very well. Much depends on how you start a class and what opportunities and invitations you extend to your students in doing so.

Simply asking your class what they thought of the assignment for the week can lead to a painful silence; that may be too big a question for most students to know how to answer right away, and they may feel that you have a particular response in mind, since you, after all, will usually have chosen the assignments you are asking about. It is better to give them something more specific to begin with. You might pass out a brief document or problem set, or read a brief passage from the assigned reading and ask for responses. You might write on the blackboard a series of questions or ideas from an earlier class or assignment. You might ask the students to write a thesis statement or topic sentence on a subject you wish to discuss and then have one or two students read their efforts aloud. Or you might simply begin with a deliberately provocative question that you feel certain will inspire disagreement.

It is useful to start any discussion with questions that can lead in multiple directions—questions that do not have a single, simple answer. Good discussions thrive on disagreement, and a question or set of questions that launches a debate will be more effective than straightforward, linear questions that lead in only one direction.

Many instructors assign students to lead, or at least launch, the discussion each week, which has the advantage of giving them an experience of thinking through the subject and trying to present ideas in class. But students may be less successful than you would be in generating discussion among their peers, so you should be prepared to step in if their efforts to stimulate participation flag. Students will often be more successful in launching a discussion if you have started the class yourself once or twice first and given them an example of the kinds of questions and classroom styles that work. They are also likely to be more successful if they are working in teams and are thus forced to have conversations about the material with one another before they try leading a conversation in the classroom.

SUSTAINING A DISCUSSION

Once the discussion has begun, even if it is proceeding smoothly on its own, students will be watching for your reactions to what they say. You may be entirely silent, but your facial expressions and body language can have a major impact on what students think about their own comments, or those of others. Positive reinforcement—smiling, nodding, complimenting—can be helpful in encouraging a discussion, although only if your encouragement is spread fairly widely around the class. You should avoid discouraging conversation with negative expressions or gestures, even inadvertent ones. In any case, you should remember that you will never be just another participant in a discussion. Your behavior—both spoken and physical—will always have a significant influence on how your class behaves and perceives itself.

Even a successful, self-sustaining conversation will require your intervention from time to time—to move the discussion in the directions you think it should go, or to rescue it from students who are taking it off track. You should be constantly alert to signs that the discussion is bogging down, becoming repetitious, or moving away from the issues you think are important. When it does, you need to step in and try to redirect it.

One of the most difficult questions facing any discussion leader is how to deal with students who are making mistakes or missing the point. You should not let misinformation or misdirection continue unanswered, but neither should you discourage or embarrass the students who are responsible for the problems. If possible, find something positive to say about even the most wrongheaded remark—"You're right about this, but wrong about that," or "That would be correct if this were true," or something of the sort—before refuting or correcting a student's comment. If a student has said something intelligent or interesting, even if incorrect, you might respond with a comment such as "That's a great wrong answer," which will encourage further discussion of the response. Sometimes, of course, students will argue with and correct each other in a discussion, and in that case the best thing for you to do is stay out of the way. But when a comment or question is directed at you, always make sure that you respond somehow—with praise, with criticism, with another question aimed at the group. And when significant errors go uncorrected, be sure to correct them—gently.

Leading a discussion often requires considerable patience. When you ask a question or raise an issue, give your students some time to think before calling on anyone to speak. Avoid calling on the first raised hand, especially if it goes up very quickly, which suggests that the student in question has not thought much about what he or she is going to say. Make sure students know that in the first moments of class a thoughtful silence is perfectly appropriate. If no one responds to a question after a few moments, ask yourself if you have framed it badly and need to refocus it. Keep rephrasing it, and adding more information, until students know enough to respond to it.

Even seemingly simple decisions can have a big impact on a discussion. For example, should you stand or sit? In a small seminar, it makes sense to sit at the table (or in a circle of chairs) with the students, to make it clear that you are all part of a conversation together—and to make your own temporary withdrawal from a lively, self-sustaining discussion easier. But with a larger or a more reticent group, especially one in which you are using Socratic methods, it often makes sense to stand and to move strategically around the room as a way of creating a sense of energy and engagement. Your physical presence can have a significant effect on a discussion. For example, if you are trying to encourage students to challenge one another, consider standing behind a student being challenged to avoid having the challenger feel torn between addressing remarks to you and addressing them to a peer.

How you use the blackboard can also affect the character of a discussion. You can use the board to chart the progress of a discussion, to draw attention to particularly important questions, to pose choices, to write passages of text to be analyzed or problems to be solved. (If you do use the blackboard, be sure that your writing is legible and is large enough to be read by the students seated furthest from it.) You can also ask students themselves to use the board to work out ideas or problems they are trying to resolve.

Some discussions, particularly in larger classes, will always be guided by the instructor. But in many cases, particularly in smaller classes, there is a different goal. A seminar instructor will usually strive to get a discussion to a place where the students, not the teacher, are in control—where there is enough commitment to the conversation, and enough interest in the questions it raises, that it can continue without you. Getting to that point can be very difficult and requires patience, flexibility, and sometimes considerable prodding. But when a discussion takes on a life of its own, stand back—at least for a while—and let it build, intervening gently only when you feel it necessary to steer the conversation back to the issues you want students to address.

REVIVING A LAGGING DISCUSSION

Even the best planned and best directed discussion can fail to take off, or can fizzle out into silence after a while. A stalled discussion is always uncomfortable for both students and teacher, and there are times when nothing you do will rekindle it effectively. But there are techniques for jump-starting a flagging discussion that will work more often than not.

One way to help ensure that your discussions do not flag irretrievably is to establish early that students should come to every class prepared to report on something: a document of their choosing, related to the topic for the week, which they are to bring with them to class; a reading journal they are asked to keep; a question they are asked to prepare. If all your students understand that they are liable to be called on without warning to give a short report on something they have brought with them, they are likely to be better prepared for class than if they feel confident that they can sit silently without fear of reproach. And if the discussion does flag, you have an immediate recourse—ask one of your students to give a quick report.

Playing the devil's advocate—taking an outrageous position on an issue to try to provoke rejoinders—can be effective in igniting a discussion, although it runs the risk of offending or confusing students. You should signal your class when you are taking this approach. Using analogies to current events or to contemporary popular culture can sometimes help; almost everyone will have something to say about a current political controversy or a currently popular film or television show. But here, too, you have to be careful; you don't want a discussion of *Moby Dick* to turn into a discussion of *Friends.*

Another approach to a faltering discussion is to ask students to read something out loud, such as a passage from the text assigned for the week or a document you (or they) have brought to class. You can then focus discussion on that for a while and hope students will pick up the thread from there. Counterfactual questions—would America have become bogged down in Vietnam if John Kennedy had lived; how would we evaluate F. Scott Fitzgerald if he had not written *The Great Gatsby;* how would the U.S. government be different if there were no Senate—can often open up new avenues of discussion. Even a simple, objective question—a question with a single, correct answer—might give students a way back into a discussion that has lost its way. All such approaches are, in effect, devices, whose principal value is in stirring students to speak. You should try not to stick with any of them for too long.

Both a successful discussion and a flagging discussion that needs reviving will often profit from many different kinds of questions, used strategically at different times depending on the circumstances. Linear questions, which can discourage discussion at the beginning of class, may help revive it later. Open-ended questions, with many possible answers, can get a discussion going; but they can also increase the tension in a room where a discussion has gone awry. It is important to learn how to use the right kinds of questions in the right places. It is also important for beginning teachers to recognize that this—like many other things—is a skill that takes time to learn. Being a successful discussion leader may not come naturally; but if you make an effort to analyze your own performance and test new techniques, you will almost certainly get better over time.

BRINGING A DISCUSSION TO AN END

The concluding moments of any class discussion are very important. You don't want a discussion simply to run out of steam or out of time. You want, rather, to lead the discussion to some kind of satisfactory conclusion that will leave students with a sense of what they have, or should have, learned. You can conclude with remarks of your own, summarizing or clarifying important points. You can ask your students to offer a summary of the arguments themselves. You can signal what you will be considering at the next meeting or what unanswered questions you will want the class to return to. But whatever you do, and however briefly you do it, you should be sure that there is a clear conclusion. Do not let the discussion simply fizzle out, or stop abruptly at the end of the period.

But do end class on time. Students have other courses and obligations, and they are rightly annoyed when an instructor keeps them late.

HELPING STUDENTS TEACH
THEMSELVES

The classroom discussion, in all its many varieties, is the most common form of teaching and learning in relatively small groups. But many instructors build out from discussions to involve their students in group work or to use other techniques which delegate more responsibility to the student. Educational theorists make a distinction between teaching and learning, and many now argue that traditional classroom methods do not do enough to make students active participants in their own learning process. Collaborative teaching and other techniques can give students a more direct role in their own education. Delegating work and authority to students does not, however, mean that your role is any less important. On the contrary, student-centered learning is highly dependent on the instructor's guidance and participation.

There are many ways to engage students in collective learning processes. One of the simplest—and a very good way to ensure that even relatively quiet students have the experience of participating in discussions—is simply to divide your class into small groups, each of which will have its own discussion about some aspect of the day's material. After a certain period of time, you can bring the class back together and ask each group to report on the results of its discussion. You can ask several groups to discuss the same question and then see what different perspectives result. Or you can ask each group to evaluate a different portion of an assignment or problem, and then try to put the different reports together at the end. You can start with one set of groups and then rescramble them to bring the perspectives of different groups into contact with one another.

While students are meeting in smaller groups, you might choose to leave the room for a while to make clear to them that they are now in charge of the learning process. You might just stand or sit to the side until the time comes for the group discussions to come to a close. You might move from group to group, listening and answering questions if any are asked, but not usually intervening otherwise and certainly not directing the discussion. (Some teachers take down phrases heard in each group and write them on the blackboard as a way to help bring the discussions together once the group reports are completed.) If you do join a group, you should sit down with the students. Standing above them while they are sitting can intimidate them and erode their sense of having control over their work.

There are many other ways of creating group activities. You can assign students to work together on some aspect of an assignment and prepare a report to deliver to the class. You can send students out together to research a question and ask them to develop materials that they can distribute or display to others. You can stage debates, mock trials, and other simulations. You can make several students responsible for launching a discussion or summarizing it at the end. You can involve students in a collective project (producing a collaborative report on an issue, creating a multiauthored journal, publishing material on the Internet), in which everyone has responsibilities to everyone else. With these and many other techniques, you can help students feel both a sense of responsibility to the class and a sense of control over their own learning.

Be sure to give students guidance in advance, so that they will understand what they are going to do and what is expected of them. You should try as well to encourage students to negotiate responsibilities among themselves when they are working on collaborative projects, and perhaps to choose a group leader or a secretary to help them organize or record their work. If the class is dividing up into groups and you know the students well enough to sense who might work well together, you may wish to make the assignments yourself. If you do not know the students well enough to feel confident in your judgment, you should probably organize the groups more or less randomly. When you allow students to form their own groups, you run the risk of putting groups of friends together, of excluding some students, or of creating racial, gender, or intellectual divisions or imbalances.

Organizing students into self-directed groups does not guarantee that all students will participate in the group's work. Some students may be as passive in a small-group effort as they are in the class as a whole; some might be even more passive, assuming that in your absence nothing important is at stake. To guard against this problem, you might insist that each member of a group participate in the group's report to the class. You might assign each student a paper based on the group work. You might design a grading system in which everyone's grade in the group is affected by the quality of everyone else's answers. (This approach also ensures that stronger students develop their own teaching skills, since they will have a stake in ensuring that everyone in their group learns and contributes something.)

SIMULATION EXERCISES

Simulations are an especially elaborate and structured form of group activity. In a simulation, students are asked to assume the roles of actors in the material they are studying: historical figures, policymakers, literary characters or critics, and so forth. They are asked to drop their accustomed roles as detached observers of the issues they are studying and become, for a time, active participants in the events or ideas they are being asked to understand. In a small way, simulations can play something of the role in the humanities and social sciences that laboratories play in the natural sciences.

If you are planning a simulation, assign students their roles in advance and make sure there is sufficient material available to allow them to understand what their characters might think or say. Before the class begins, you might have each student write a paper based on his or her character or role. When you return it, you can include suggestions for additional reading and preparation. By the time the in-class simulation begins, students should have spent considerable time preparing for it. When the simulation is complete, you might have all students write a paper based on the exercise. These papers will help them step back and make sense of the usually unfamiliar experience they have just had. They will also help you get a sense of how successful the simulation was.

Popular simulations include such things as impeachment trials of presidents who were never impeached, debates over Constitutional amendments which were never proposed, discussions by writers of their work even though no record of such discussions may exist, or discussions by literary characters of their motives. Simulations can also attempt to recreate real events, but with no expectation that the simulation will replicate reality. A simulated Constitutional Convention might well end up without a Senate, or with a prime minister instead of a president.

There are commercially packaged simulations, usually in the form of games, but you will be more successful if you design a simulation yourself, or in collaboration with your students. Focus on important issues. Simulations are time consuming, so don't waste them on questions or material you consider unimportant. Involve all students at all times in the simulation. Do not, for example, make some students witnesses and others jurors in a trial. That will guarantee that some are passive observers for most of the activity. Make them play both witnesses and jurors. If you assign papers in advance as preparation for a simulation, read and return them to the students before the activity begins. When you assign roles in the simulation, consider asking students to "play against type," for example by requiring a conservative student to take the part of a radical. And make sure that the materials to support the simulation are readily available in your library, on the Internet, or through other sources (including forms that you can distribute yourself).

You should not intervene very much during a simulation, although you might want to create small windows from time to time where you can comment on the proceedings. Students should be allowed to make mistakes, and you should be reasonably tolerant of an exercise that is not going as planned. But if a simulation (or any other independent group activity) goes badly awry, or breaks down altogether—either because of inadequate preparation by you or the students, or because of some unforeseen difficulty—don't be afraid to break in to try to reignite it, or even to put it out of its misery.

DEBATES AND PANEL DISCUSSIONS

Classroom debates or panel discussions may be more familiar to you and to your students than simulations. They are also easier to organize. But many of the same techniques are useful here as well. As with a simulation, the critical factor is the choice of topic. Choose something students will find important or exciting. Give students a chance to prepare, either individually or in teams. Do not create debates in which large numbers of students are passive observers for long periods. During the debate itself, give nonparticipating students chances to ask questions of the participants. Leave time at the end for the class as a whole to assess the results.

Whatever topic you pick, you should consider having students produce some sort of short paper before the activity and a second short paper after it. Without closure students will listen politely to the other presentations but will never have a reason to take close notes or to rethink the arguments made in class.

OTHER FORMS OF
COLLABORATIVE LEARNING

The examples presented here are only a few of the many ways in which students can be encouraged to play a more active role in learning than many traditional forms of teaching provide. Some of the most important collaborative learning experiences can occur outside the classroom: students can be assigned to engage in joint research projects, to produce short films or videos together, to create a class journal. The Internet can facilitate important new forms of learning as well, by making it possible for students actually to publish the results of their work. (Chapter 10 offers suggestions on how to use the Internet and other electronic tools.) You or your students may discover other forms of self-generated or collaborative learning as you move through the term. In fact, one of the best ways to encourage such learning is to include students in the process of conceiving and planning it.

Handing responsibility for learning over to the students can yield enormous rewards of excitement, engagement, and innovation. But every instructor, every group of students, and every body of material is different. Be careful to adjust your techniques and your expectations to your own circumstances. And be prepared to step in and provide some direction to the class when circumstances require it.

FOUR

THE ART AND
CRAFT OF
LECTURING

Delivering lectures is one of the oldest forms of teaching at the college and university level and is still, perhaps, the most common. It has many critics. Some educational theorists argue that lectures are passive experiences for students and undermine their efforts to become actively engaged in the learning process. Others argue that lectures are obsolete, that they simply present in spoken form material that can be more effectively presented in written (including electronic) form and distributed to students.

But lecturing has survived generations of criticism and is likely to survive many more. One reason is simple economics. Large colleges and universities often do not have the resources to permit all teaching to be conducted in intimate classes where discussion and active student participation are the norm. But there are other, and better, justifications for lecturing as a valuable form of teaching as well.

A series of lectures is a form of pedagogy that has no counterpart elsewhere. It represents a teacher's effort to understand a large body of knowledge, synthesize it, and present it to students in a way that he or she believes makes sense. It is, at its best, a thematic exercise, in which the lecturer makes conscious and deliberate choices about what kinds of material to discuss and what meaning to assign to it. And it is an extended exercise. A typical lecture course requires an instructor to present twenty to thirty lectures in a term, which in turn produces a steady accumulation of information and, ideally, a clearly charted path through the material—from a starting point to a conclusion. Most of all, perhaps, lectures create a certain chemistry, and at their best they can be as intellectually stimulating, even exciting, to students as the liveliest discussion or the most engrossing collaborative activity. They can also be an invaluable learning experience for the teacher giving them, because preparing and delivering lectures forces you to explain to yourself—before you try to explain to others—what you think is most important about your field and why it is significant.

Delivering your first lecture, and giving your first lecture course, can be a very intimidating process and will certainly involve a great deal of work. The onerous demands of preparing two or three lectures a week would be trying enough by themselves. But this difficult preparation coincides with a teacher's effort to master a form of activity that is, in many cases, entirely new. Few instructors have much if any experience in delivering lectures before they are called upon to offer a lecture course of their own. They must learn on the job.

Perhaps more than any other kind of teaching, lecturing puts the personality and the intellect of the teacher on display. It is, in a sense, a very personal kind of teaching, because in most cases it is you, much more than the students, who determine the nature of the classroom experience. You need to think carefully, therefore, about what kind of lecturing works best for you: what kinds of preparations you wish to make, what style of presentation you wish to use, and to what degree you want to encourage your students to participate in the lecturing process. You will probably find yourself experimenting with a number of different styles and techniques before you find the ones that are best for you. Most teachers remember lecturers they themselves encountered as students and will be tempted to borrow styles and techniques from those they admired. That is both natural and, often, helpful. But you should keep in mind that what worked for your teachers may not work for you. As much as in any other kind of teaching, lecturing needs to fit comfortably with your own temperament and personality.

PREPARING A LECTURE

A lecture depends heavily on the style of its presentation, to be sure. But it is, at its heart, a way of conveying ideas and information to your students. Even the most stylishly and engagingly presented lecture will be of little value if it does not contain real substance, and if it does not challenge students to think. The most important part of lecturing, therefore, is done before you ever enter the classroom: preparing and organizing your own ideas about your subject.

In preparing a lecture, you should think first of a question, or group of questions, you want to try to answer, and of how the material you are considering in one lecture relates to the others you have given or will give. A lecture should not be simply a narrative or an assemblage of factual material. It should contain an argument, and the material you present should be organized to support and advance the argument. That does not mean that a lecture must be linear, with every passage moving relentlessly toward a single conclusion. There can be digressions, secondary arguments, anecdotes, jokes, and stories along the way. But when you reach the end of the class, students should have a sense of where you have taken them and why. Like a discussion, a lecture should not simply trail off when the bell rings. It should have a conclusion that draws your argument to an effective end and, perhaps, points ahead to what is coming next.

In structuring your lecture, keep in mind that you are speaking to an audience with very particular needs and expectations. They will want to know how the contents of your lecture fit in with other elements of your course—readings, papers, class discussions. They will want to know how each lecture follows the one preceding it or leads into the one following it. Most of all, they will want to take notes; and to do so effectively, they will need to be able to follow your argument easily and to recognize what is most important about it. Your lectures can be flamboyant, idiosyncratic, speculative, or fanciful. But whatever else they are, they should also be carefully and transparently organized. The central points need to be emphasized, and repeated, so that students are always clear about why you are covering the material you have chosen. (Repetition is usually something to avoid; but in lectures, repetition—particularly repetition of critical points—can often be valuable.) Without clear and explicit guidance, students will spend much of the class puzzling over what is important and how to take notes rather than listening to what you have to say.

Putting together a lecture, especially when you don't have very much experience at it, is a daunting task. It is not the same as writing a paper, an article, or a book. Unless you are lecturing on something which you yourself have researched extensively, an opportunity which will arise relatively infrequently for most people, you will have to rely on the work of others. You should feel no obligation to be wholly original. There is no reason for hesitation in borrowing material, even ideas, from articles, books, even other lectures—although you should not borrow specific language, and you should give credit to others when you are echoing particularly distinctive ideas borrowed from another source. When you are preparing two or three lectures a week over the course of a term, you will need all the help you can get; and the synthetic efforts of other people can often be of enormous value to you. Obviously, when all is said and done, a lecture should reflect your own ideas and interests and should not simply duplicate someone else's work. But those ideas and interests, more often than not, will have their origins in what you have read by others; and your lectures will inevitably reflect that.

Once you have decided on the topic and the broad argument of a lecture, spend some time reading or rereading material on your subject that you think is interesting and useful. If the subject is relatively new to you, you will probably not have time to read extensively; look for works that have already synthesized material on your topic, or that summarize the state of a field, or that fit your subject into a larger narrative. Take notes on the material and, as you are doing so, begin imagining how you will put it together for presentation to your class. When you have done enough reading (or when you have run out of time to do any more), begin organizing the material.

A lecture should not be simply a collection of facts, but even in such largely abstract fields as philosophy or linguistics, it should not be entirely conceptual either. Most students require concrete examples and illustrations to make arguments seem vivid and persuasive to them, and in most lectures you should be sure to have appropriate material available to support or illustrate your argument. Quoting from contemporary statements and documents—the more vivid and dramatic the better—is one good way to give concrete form to an argument. Another is to tell an illustrative story or to create a hypothetical example. Visual aids such as slides, film clips, and so on, can do a great deal to add substance and detail to your lectures. Experienced lecturers are always on the lookout for bits of material—passages of text, humorous or dramatic stories, personal anecdotes, newspaper or magazine articles, scholarly papers, interpretive or synthetic essays—that might help enrich or enliven their lectures. When you find such material you should be sure to file or record it in some way (preferably with your lecture notes) so that it will be available to you when you return to a lecture topic. Striking a balance between illustrative material that is entertaining and illuminating and the argument the material is meant to advance is one of the most important tasks you will face.

LECTURING FROM TEXTS, NOTES, OR MEMORY

One question all lecturers confront early on is what kind of notes will work best for them. Should you write out a full text of your lecture and have it in front of you in class? Should you simply make an outline or notes, and if so how extensive should they be? Should you speak without notes, and if so how should you prepare yourself for doing so? Making such choices will require you to think about, or discover, what works best for you. Each approach has advantages and disadvantages.

Many lecturers write out full texts of their lectures, and there are a number of good reasons for doing so. Writing a lecture out is the only way to be entirely sure you have worked through exactly what you want to say and how you want to say it; even the most extensive notes may leave you with some knotty problem unanticipated and unresolved and force you to struggle to deal with it while standing before your class; a finished text will require you to make such decisions in advance. Writing out lectures is also valuable in helping you fit your presentation into the time available. Once you have figured out how rapidly you can comfortably speak (which for most people is between two and three minutes per double-spaced page), you can use your written text to gauge the length of your lecture and adjust it to fit the time you have. Another advantage of writing out lectures is that they provide you with protection against some of the vicissitudes of teaching. All instructors have bad days, when they are tired, distracted, ill, or for some other reason not at their best. Delivering a lecture can be extremely difficult under such circumstances, particularly if you are depending heavily on your memory and imagination to do so. Having a text in front of you can be an indispensable crutch on days when you lack the creative energy to do it on your own. Finally, writing out your lectures can be very useful in future years, when you return to a course, in providing you with a full record of what you have done and a starting point for doing it again.

But there are also disadvantages to written texts. Some lecturers can stand in a classroom, read a polished text, and sound as though they are speaking informally. But many others find it impossible to read a text without sounding formal and stilted and remote. If you cannot read a text smoothly and engagingly, and if you cannot comfortably digress from it or adjust it as you go along and as ideas occur to you, then you probably should not have one in front of you or, if you do, you should refer to it for guidance only when you need it but try not to read it. Written texts can also be addictive. They can tempt instructors to give the same lecture again and again, year after year. Stories of professors teaching from yellowed lecture notes are staples of academic mythology, but there is enough truth in them to serve as a warning.

For lecturers who feel uncomfortable with a written text, or who do not think it is worth the time to prepare one, a combination of an outline and notes often serves many of the same purposes—and sometimes serves them better. If your outline is sufficiently careful and detailed, and if you have integrated into it a full enough indication of what kinds of illustrations you want to use and what kinds of arguments you want to make, then you may well realize many of the advantages of both a text (a full and well-developed structure and plan) and spontaneity (speaking to some degree extemporaneously and dynamically). Notes and outlines can be of any length and detail, of course, from a few notes on a single page to an elaborate document nearly as long as a written text. Indeed, some lecturers create notes that are nearly identical to a written text, but without fully formed sentences—

to require them to extemporize to some degree as they deliver the lecture. Only experience will tell you how elaborate your notes must be to enable you to lecture at your best, or whether you will do better with a fully written text.

Finally, some lecturers prefer to lecture with no notes at all, or with such minimal notes that they are in effect speaking without any significant written assistance. This is a very dangerous approach for a beginning lecturer, but at times a very rewarding one for more experienced teachers. To lecture successfully without notes requires a combination of a reliable memory—so that you will be able to recall your plan for the lecture as you go along—and an ability to be clear and articulate when speaking spontaneously. Lecturing well without notes usually requires at least as much preparation as any other kind of lecturing—and sometimes much more. But however well prepared you are, you will still find yourself standing in a classroom with nothing to fall back on if your memory or imagination fail you on any given day. If you find you are good at it, however, lecturing without notes can also be exhilarating for you and exciting for your students, who almost always notice when a lecturer is speaking extemporaneously and are usually very impressed when it is done well.

DELIVERING A LECTURE

How you deliver a lecture will depend on many things: the size of your class, the character of your classroom, and most of all your own personal style. But there are guidelines that can help you decide how to present your material whatever the circumstances.

Some are obvious. Speak loudly and forcefully (using a microphone if necessary in a large room), both to ensure that everyone in the room can hear you and so that you do not seem tentative or unsure. If you are a first-time lecturer, you will certainly be nervous. But you can obscure a great deal of your own anxiety simply by speaking emphatically and clearly. Look directly at your audience as much as possible, and do not gaze only at one part of the room; avoid keeping your eyes glued to your notes, and avoid gazing at the ceiling or the floor or the wall or out the window.

Don't speak too fast. Even if you are running out of time, be sure to speak in a deliberate and unrushed way. Remember that students are taking notes and will be unable to do so effectively if you are rushed. If you have to, discard material (you can often use it later), or simply cut the lecture short (you can finish it next time). The best way to avoid rushing to finish a lecture, however, is to prepare it carefully to fit the time available to you. Don't speak in a monotone. Change your inflections and even your pace as you move from one kind of statement to another. And finish on time. It is both irritating and inconsiderate to your students to keep them late. Many of them will have other classes or obligations.

The physical conditions under which you lecture are also important. You will probably have little control over the character of the classroom in which you teach, but you should do your best to make certain that it meets a few minimal conditions. Obviously, your classroom should be large enough to accommodate your students so that everyone has a seat; ideally, there should be at least 20 percent more seats than there are students. But the room should not be too large. A very big lecture hall for a small class creates a strange and disheartening atmosphere for students and teacher. If you use a text or substantial notes, you should have a lectern on which to place them. Spreading your notes out on a table top makes them hard to see, forces you to spend too much time looking down, and can distract your students. If you plan to use the blackboard, make sure it is accessible and large enough and that there is chalk and an eraser. Make sure the room is adequately lit. Students will be very discouraged if they have trouble seeing the blackboard or their own notes.

Finally, if you are using audiovisual or computer aids, make sure the room is equipped to handle them.

Although the most important purpose of a lecture is to help students learn, there is no reason it cannot also be entertaining. Even the most abstract and theoretical subject can be made more interesting to students if from time to time you digress from your central argument and throw in stories, anecdotes, and even jokes. The more engaging your presentation is, the more students will pay attention to its substance. But be careful not to overdo it. A few jokes and anecdotes can be very helpful; too many might lead students not to take you as seriously as you would like, and even to dismiss you as an entertainer rather than a teacher.

A difficult question is how much of your self you should put into your lectures. Should you tell personal anecdotes, recount personal experiences, describe personal circumstances? If you feel uncomfortable talking about yourself publicly, then of course there is no need to do so. But an occasional personal story, assuming it is interesting or amusing and is in some way relevant to your subject, can humanize both you and your lecture. Do not, however, allow a lecture to become the occasion for elaborate explorations of your personal history.

There are other techniques that some lecturers use to help make their points. You can distribute documents, maps, charts, or tables to students as they walk in so that you can discuss detailed information without having to take valuable time presenting it. (You can also present the same material through slides, overhead projection, computer projection, or simply the blackboard.) You can write important names or terms on the blackboard so that students will have easy access to them (and their spelling). You can write an outline of your lecture on the board, or project it by overhead projector, to help guide students through your spoken presentation. (The minds of even the most dedicated students wander at times; an outline can help students reconnect with the lecture if they have temporarily drifted away.)

In the end, however, the success of a lecture depends on its content, and on your ability to deliver it convincingly. There is no single formula for doing that. Some lecturers pace the room and lecture in an animated way; others remain relatively still. Some are witty and humorous, others serious. Some use a great many visual aids, and others use none. The only things that all successful lecturers have in common is being clear and articulate, being organized, and being engaged.

ENCOURAGING STUDENT PARTICIPATION

A lecture need not be a passive experience for your students. At the simplest level, the act of taking notes is itself an active involvement with your material, which requires students to summarize what you are saying and make choices about what is important. But many lecturers encourage students to participate in more direct ways. When your class is relatively small, it is easy to combine lecturing with discussion—to move in and out of your own presentation by asking students questions or eliciting their reactions. Even when the class is large, a lecturer can sometimes use Socratic methods to draw students into a discussion or simply solicit questions from the students.

As in any other class, your physical movements can make a big difference in a lecture, particularly if you are trying to draw students into a discussion. If you normally stand behind a lectern in order to see your notes, move away from it when you are engaging with students, to signal to them that the relative formality of the actual lecture is giving way to a more informal exchange. If you are standing behind a large table, walk around to the front of it, sit on it, even walk into the aisle to address students who are asking questions or are responding to yours.

Keep in mind that in a large class, especially in a very large one, many students will be nervous when they ask or respond to questions. Be careful not to embarrass them, even inadvertently. Never make fun of a student's comment; don't laugh at anything your students say (unless what they say is intended to be funny); don't encourage anyone else to laugh at them either. Humiliating a student in public is something no teacher should ever do, both because it is an abuse of your authority and because it will virtually ensure that the student in question, and many others, will never speak in your class again.

When to encourage student interventions is an important issue, and one you should think about carefully before you begin to do so. Some lecturers encourage students to interrupt whenever they have questions. This might work well in a small class, in which the lecture is closely integrated with discussion. It can also work well in a larger class if the questions are not too frequent or distracting. But a lecture, more than a seminar or a discussion, is designed to present information and ideas to all your students; if a few voluble students begin interrupting frequently to ask questions that may be of little interest to the rest of the class, you will not be able to do what you need to do. You will also begin to lose the attention of the rest of the class.

Some lecturers try to save some time at the end of class for questions. That is not always easy to do, since you will often have difficulty fitting your lecture into the available period and will not have any time to spare. But if you have the time, encouraging questions at the end of your lecture will give students a sense that they can probe further into what you said without interrupting your presentation. If you are going to leave time for questions, make sure students know that in advance so that they can be thinking about what they might like to ask you as you speak.

Other lecturers begin each class by asking students if they have questions about the previous lecture. You might give them a minute or two to review their notes, but once you have established a pattern of soliciting questions at the start you will probably find that some students come prepared with them. You will, of course, need to shorten your lecture to offset the time spent on questions, but be careful not to allow questions to go on so long as to make it difficult for you to cover the material you have prepared for the day.

Still other lecturers incorporate student comments into the lecture itself by asking a series of questions of the audience, the answers to which will advance the argument of the lecture and also give students a sense of some of the intellectual questions that go into making a scholarly judgment. You should think carefully in advance about when in your lecture you wish to involve the audience, and where you want that involvement to lead. You should be careful, as well, not to allow the exchange with your students to stray from the points you want to illuminate or continue longer than you think is appropriate.

Student participation in lectures can be very valuable both to you and to them. But in the end, a lecture is primarily for the purpose of instructing, and whatever interaction you encourage should help you make the points you wish to make. In many other kinds of classes, student participation is to some degree an end in itself. In a lecture, it usually is not.

Most college and university lecturers will find themselves doing considerable lecturing whether they like it, or believe in it, or not. Giving a good lecture is, like most other teaching, a combination of art and craft. It provides you with many opportunities for creative expression, for imaginative presentation, and for projecting personal charisma. But even if you are not a naturally gifted lecturer, even if you feel you lack the intangible talents that can make lecturing a kind of art, you can deliver successful, highly effective lectures if you prepare carefully and work over time to find a style of presentation that is both comfortable for you and engaging to your students.

The research paper or independent project is often the part of the learning process that students remember most clearly and from which they derive the most lasting benefits. That is because it is usually the part of the process for which they are themselves most fully responsible and in which they can best pursue interests of their own.

There are many courses—and even some entire disciplines—in which independent assignments are impractical or inappropriate. But in some courses, the independent assignment can and should be a central part, even the most important part, of your curriculum. Obviously, it requires the same kind of careful planning and thought you should give to any other important part of your teaching. If treated as a casual afterthought, it can become a confusing burden to students. It can also be a consuming chore for the teacher, who at the end of the term will face a flood of visits from panicky students searching desperately at the last minute for topics and, not long after that, the dismal task of evaluating an imposing pile of dreary essays. (Providing insufficient guidance for students undertaking a daunting and, for many, unfamiliar task can also invite plagiarism.) But if integrated carefully into your course, it can become an invaluable extension of it, and a way to cultivate vital skills and a greater appreciation of the subject. Most of all, it can help students discover a way to learn independently and to feel in control of their own work.

RELATING PROJECTS TO YOUR COURSE

Once you have decided to include an independent project in your course, consider whether you want it to supplement or complement the rest of the curriculum. In other words, do you want the project to explore topics that you do not intend to cover but still consider significant, or do you want it to reinforce subjects that you already plan to address in depth? There are advantages to both approaches.

A supplementary project—a project in which students examine issues and material they do not otherwise encounter in class—is the most truly independent kind of assignment, and it places a premium not just on researching and writing a paper, but on finding a way to identify and define a topic. It is also the more difficult approach to an independent assignment, and to some students tremendously intimidating.

A complementary project—one that is closely tied to the central themes of the course—may stimulate class discussions, deepen understanding of issues you consider important, and permit students to pursue topics with which they have some familiarity because they have already spent time on them in class. It also makes it possible for you to identify clearly what research or other materials students should use, and it relieves them (and you) of the difficult task of identifying topics on their own. But it also makes the paper less fully their own, cuts them off from the possibility of examining material in which they are interested but that your course does not cover, and makes it less likely that any paper will be truly original.

It is not always necessary for you to choose between

these two approaches. You can give the choice to your students. They can choose between writing a paper drawn from a list of topics you have devised for them, which are closely tied to the rest of the course, or proposing a topic of their own. Students intimidated by the thought of finding their own topics will likely gravitate to the former. Bolder students, or those with strong preexisting interests, will be more likely to choose the latter.

GUIDING STUDENTS INTO INDEPENDENT PROJECTS

Students who set out to write traditional research papers on topics of their own choosing may need to be told a number of things that are self-evident to you. One is the difference between a "subject" (an area of interest) and a "topic" (something specific and containable enough that it can be managed within the confines of the time and resources available to them). Students may be interested in, for example, race relations in modern America; but that is not, of course, a topic for a paper. How black and white newspapers portrayed the riot in Watts in 1965, on the other hand, is a topic that a student with access to a good library can probably handle.

For a topic to be appropriate, there must be sources that will enable your students to examine it effectively. Very early in the process of choosing a topic, students should spend enough time exploring potential sources to have a sense of the practical possibilities for research. If the appropriate sources do not exist, or are not realistically available to them, then they will need to make some adjustments—perhaps even consider a new topic altogether.

Students also need to know that a successful paper includes not simply information, but a thesis that is neither self-evident nor insupportable. They need to marshal evidence from a respectable range of sources, craft a coherent argument, and present it in clear and, ideally, elegant prose. They need to know what constitutes plagiarism and how to avoid it. And they need help from you in all these areas.

One way to help students find their way into topics is to ask them to submit a short written proposal well in advance of the date papers are due. That will encourage them to begin thinking about their topics. It will also give them, and you, a chance to see if their ideas make sense when committed to paper. You can return their proposals with comments or suggestions, arrange meetings with them to discuss the proposals, or engage the entire class in commenting on each other's ideas and making suggestions.

Where students will be most in need of your help is in suggesting sources. In some cases that will not be much easier for you than it is for them. Students who choose their own topics will very often pick something about which you know little or nothing. There is no reason to hide that from them, just as there is no reason to discourage them from pursuing a topic with which you are unfamiliar. But even if you do not know very much about specific sources, you should be able to give them some general guidance about how to identify sources: what kinds of indexes and electronic search devices they can use; which secondary works are likely to help them; which librarians they might ask for assistance. Explain to them the usefulness of footnotes and bibliographies in relevant existing works for identifying sources. Even when a student is writing on a topic you know a great deal about, do not give so much advice as to foreclose independent discoveries. Provide guidance, of course, but leave room for the student to chart a course on his or her own.

OTHER KINDS OF PAPERS

If a full-scale, independent research paper does not seem appropriate for your students or your course, there are other

kinds of written work that can serve some of the same purposes. One is the *primary source paper*, through which you can
give students experience in the critical use of written and visual sources. Have students select (on their own or with your
assistance) a single text, or several, for close analysis. In literary fields, that might mean making use of whatever critical
theory you are encouraging them to master. In history and
other more empirical fields, it may mean asking them to consider the origins or impact of the text. In such cases, you
might ask students to consider some or all of the following
questions in preparing their papers:

- What was the viewpoint, motivation, potential
  bias, and intended audience of the author or
  artist?
- In what social climate and context was the cultural product created?
- What was its intended "message"? How effectively was it presented?

Encourage students to reinforce their arguments with evidence from class notes, assigned readings, or other sources.

Another approach to writing assignments is the *review
essay*, which has two common forms. This, too, will likely
take very different shapes in different disciplines. One kind
of review essay is *contextual*. An example would be asking
students to choose (either on their own or from a list you
provide) a book, film, play, or other cultural text that had
some impact on its age or has subsequently come to seem
representative of its time to later generations, such as Betty
Friedan's *The Feminine Mystique,* the musical *Hair,* or Jean
Renoir's *The Grand Illusion.* Ask them to analyze the meaning
and measure the effects of their selection by examining it
closely and combining their general knowledge of the period
with information gleaned from contemporary reviews and
later criticism, biographies of or articles about the creator,
or other sources. You might provide them with models for
this kind of paper (which will likely be unfamiliar to them)

by showing them examples of successful efforts from previous classes or by finding published examples—retrospective or commemorative essays on the anniversary of a book or film, for example, or on the death of a writer or artist, which sometimes appear in serious magazines or newspapers.

The *critical review* allows students to select a significant scholarly or literary work (or some group of such works) and assess the arguments. You might wish students to prepare a review without reference to anything but the text itself. You might also encourage them to familiarize themselves with other reviews or criticism from scholarly journals, popular periodicals, and major newspapers as benchmarks. This is in some ways a less challenging assignment, and, particularly if they are reading other criticism, it may encourage students to substitute, wittingly or not, the ideas and opinions of others for their own. But it does help introduce students to scholarly work and scholarly criticism—to the world you inhabit and through which you present your own ideas to them. It can help demystify scholarship and reinforce the contested character of most scholarly work.

In addition to primary source papers and review essays, you may find one or more of the following types of writing assignments to be particularly well suited to your course.

Policy memos often work well as short complementary assignments in some disciplines. They are equally effective as preparation or closure for in-class activities like debates, discussions, and simulations. If you are discussing a particular historical, political, or even literary controversy in class, encourage students to write a short paper staking out a position on the issue. By removing the need to develop an original thesis, you permit students to concentrate on building a persuasive argument, with logical assertions and relevant evidence from whatever sources you have provided or identified. The students can then transfer that skill to other assignments that demand more independent initiative on their part.

Personal journals (also known as reading logs or diaries) are running commentaries on reading or other course work, which students keep throughout the term. At some point you should collect these journals, if only to ensure that your students actually keep them, and you might consider giving them a formal grade. The value of such assignments, however, is that it keeps students writing and, ideally, forces them to think seriously about what they are learning. To help you assess and reinforce your students' note-taking skills, you may want to have the journals contain lecture notes and reading summaries as well.

Oral histories can be a valuable and exciting project in history courses, and in many others. But make sure that students do not confront the assignment unarmed. Help them become comfortable with the process of interviewing a source—perhaps by demonstrating interviewing techniques yourself or by having them interview one another in class. (A good published resource is *Doing Oral History*, by Donald Ritchie.) Advise students not to organize their paper around the interview; the interview is a source, not a subject. Suggest that they first create an outline based on secondary research and then use the information from the personal interview to substantiate or challenge the written record. Ask students to compare the different types of sources they use. Have them assess critically the strengths and weaknesses of both scholarly versions of events and the memories of contemporaries when they conflict.

Above all, remember that no single assignment works best in all situations with all students. Each has its own particular advantages and limitations. Picking the right one (or ones) requires that you consider what skills you want the students to acquire, what will engage them, what type of paper will stretch—but not overwhelm—their abilities, and what will best fit the content and format of the course.

SINGLE OR MULTIPLE PAPERS

In planning your course, you will need to decide not just what kind of papers to assign but also how many. Your decision should depend on how central writing and research are to your course, and how much other work you expect of your students during the term.

Assigning one large paper allows you to assume a more active role in the various stages of creation, from supervising rough drafts to holding personal conferences, although only if you make a concerted effort. It also gives your students the opportunity to undertake a more substantial and potentially more rewarding learning exercise than a series of shorter papers would afford them. But a single major research paper may also overwhelm weaker students, whose needs may not become apparent until too late.

Assigning several smaller essays allows you to give students more feedback over the course of the term and to vary the types of writing required. It also reduces the pressure on any one grade and prepares students for activities and discussions you have planned. But it may reduce the chance for students to revise and polish a significant piece of writing, and it may also reduce your opportunity to guide them through the process. It may be a less challenging and rewarding exercise in the end.

There are, naturally, other options. For example, you can assign a short paper at the beginning of the term and a longer paper toward the end. Assigning a brief paper in the first week or two of classes has several advantages. It requires the students to play an active role in the course from the start. It gives you an early opportunity to evaluate your students' writing and thus what kind of help they will need from you. And, if properly structured, it can give students an early chance to test some of the skills that you might ask of them in a longer assignment later on. For example, if you plan to ask students to do primary research for a substantial research paper, you might give them an early assignment to write a short essay analyzing a few primary documents.

SETTING STANDARDS AND DEADLINES FOR WRITING

Regardless of the type of assignments you decide to make, you need to give students guidance about what you expect from them. Explain your expectations and standards clearly, and early; and while some flexibility may be appropriate, you should try to stick to your guidelines as much as possible to ensure that students take them seriously.

The first questions most students will ask are very practical ones. How long should the paper be? What format do you require? When is the paper due? How much will it count? Those are relatively easy questions to answer if you have given some thought to them before you give students the assignment.

The length of an assigned paper depends on many things: the number of papers you are assigning and the amount of other work you expect; the ability and experience of your students; the kind of paper or papers you are asking them to write; and the norms of your institution. For a substantial independent paper, it is reasonable to expect students to write at least ten pages and—depending on the course and the students—sometimes up to twenty-five pages. The longer the paper, of course, the less time there will be for students to do other work in the course. So avoid assigning a paper of twenty pages or more unless it is to be the principal obligation for the class. Other kinds of papers can range from one or two pages to ten to fifteen. Whatever you decide, make it clear to the students at the beginning of the term.

Make clear, too, if you have a particular format you wish students to use. It is not unreasonable to ask that all papers be typed and double-spaced. Beyond that, you should consider whether you want students to provide footnotes, endnotes, or some other formal method of citation; whether you want a bibliography; whether you want a summary or abstract at the beginning or the end. Any such requirements, of course, create an obligation on your part to explain how to meet them. Footnotes, endnotes, and bibliographies, in particular, need considerable explanation and illustration (and, where possible, access to a good style guide, such as *The Chicago Manual of Style* or Kate Turabian's *A Manual for Writers of Term Papers, Theses, and Dissertations* or *A Student's Guide for Writing College Papers*).

Think carefully about when you want the paper to be due, and in doing so consider the schedule for the rest of the course and for other events at your institution. Explain fairly early what your policy is for late papers. If you are willing to grant extensions, state a clear and consistent policy and don't deviate from it. When a student asks for an extension, establish a new due date at the start (and keep a record of it). If you plan to penalize lateness (and you should if you expect students to respect the deadlines), make clear precisely what the penalties will be and under what circumstances they will be imposed—and make no exceptions. Penalties are usually appropriate if a student hands in a paper late without having arranged for an extension, or if a student does not adhere to a new due date that you have jointly established. In general, some flexibility on due dates is usually a good idea, since most students are juggling many obligations. But make sure that the flexibility is not arbitrary, that you have made your rules clear.

Almost all students are highly grade conscious, and how

much a paper weighs in the calculation of the course grade will have a considerable impact on how much time and attention they devote to it. If you think the papers in your course are important, weight them heavily. But whatever you decide, make clear at the beginning—ideally in the syllabus—how much the papers will count.

SUPERVISING WORK ON PAPERS

Setting guidelines does not just mean announcing expectations and requirements. It also means helping your students plan and execute their projects. If you are assigning a research paper based on primary sources, for example, spend some time in class talking about what a primary source is and how it can be used. If you are asking students to write a review essay based on secondary sources, give an example of what such an essay might look like. If you want students to write a contextual essay about a book or other document, choose an example and show how they might approach setting it in context. And help students learn how to identify and locate sources. If it is logistically possible, and if you suspect your students have little previous research experience, you might arrange for a tour of your institution's library. Librarians are usually eager to introduce students to their collections, so don't hesitate to ask them for help.

Guiding students through their projects is not a one-time exercise. You should return to the subject of the papers frequently during the term. You should also, to the degree that your own schedule permits, encourage or require students to schedule individual conferences with you to discuss their work. Such conferences allow you to monitor their progress and to help them with any problems they encounter. Finally, you should encourage students to help one another. For example, you can devote some class time to having students comment on one another's projects. Or you can organize your class into editorial groups, in which students begin critiquing one another's work early in the term and continue to do so until the end. The more collaboration you encourage in class, the more students are likely to talk with and help one another outside of class.

AVOIDING AND DEALING WITH PLAGIARISM

Few academic infractions are more serious than plagiarism— and yet few subjects are more difficult for some students to understand. Plagiarism is also a difficult issue for teachers to address, since talking about it with your students can lead them to believe that you don't trust them. But if you are concerned about plagiarism, and in most cases you probably should be, you should address it frontally, and early—taking care not to imply that you expect it to be a problem and explaining to your students that you simply want to make sure that they understand what is and is not appropriate in using the work of others. With plagiarism, preventive measures are worth far more than a punitive cure.

The easiest kind of plagiarism to explain, and the one that most students will most readily understand, is simple copying. Almost everyone understands that it is wrong to submit a paper written by someone else, or to write a paper by copying passages verbatim out of other works. And yet some students, of course, engage in this kind of plagiarism— aided today by paper-writing services and various opportunities for copying papers provided by the Internet. Sometimes it is impossible for a teacher to detect papers that are created in this way—although the more you craft a topic that is particular to your course, the smaller the chance that your students will be able to find someone else's work to borrow.

A somewhat more difficult kind of dishonesty to explain

is, in effect, self-plagiarism. In most institutions, it is improper for students to submit a paper they have written in one course to fulfill an assignment in another—unless, of course, they get the permission of both instructors involved. Otherwise, a student could, theoretically, recycle a few papers over and over again. Make clear to your students that the work they submit should not only be their own, but should be work created specifically for your course.

The most difficult issue to explain is how to deal with ideas and material derived from other sources. It will probably be clear to your students that when they borrow language from another source, they should place it in quotation marks and provide a citation—but don't take it for granted that they know that. It will probably be less clear to them what to do with ideas they have drawn from other sources, even if they express them in their own language. Explain to them that there is nothing wrong with borrowing ideas as long as they cite the source of them. And suggest that they ask themselves regularly whether they would have developed this idea without the source in front of them. If not, then they should give an attribution for it, which will simultaneously buttress their argument and provide proof of research.

Rules for citing factual information are murkier still. Students should understand that no citation is necessary for what is, in effect, common knowledge or information retrievable in standard reference sources. But information that comes from more specialized sources and that could not be readily retrieved elsewhere should always be cited. In the end, the best rule is, When in doubt, cite it.

If you think someone has committed plagiarism despite your warnings, be sure you are on firm ground before confronting the student. First, make sure you understand your institution's rules, if any, for dealing with plagiarism. It may be that all such accusations must be referred to another body, that the institution does not permit instructors to make decisions on such charges themselves. If a response is up to you, make a copy of the paper for your records. Find the source from which you believe the student has borrowed and compare it to the student's work. When you confront the student with it, give him a chance to explain his side of the story. Remember that an accusation of plagiarism is a serious matter that, if sustained, can have major consequences for a student's future, so do not make such an accusation lightly. And do not treat all plagiarism equally. You should, for example, deal differently with accidental plagiarism (such as insufficient paraphrasing or citation) than with intentional plagiarism. But if you suspect a violation of this central rule of academic life, it is your responsibility to confront it.

EVALUATING AND GRADING WRITTEN WORK

Even when papers are good, evaluating and grading them can be a long and tedious ordeal. But little that you do will be more important to—or more clearly remembered by—your students than the way you respond to their written work. So be sure to allocate sufficient time for reading and grading. Try to work on papers in a comfortable place at a relatively tranquil time. And keep in mind always that you are responding to something that may be of great personal and intellectual importance to your students. Remember how much time they have put into the project—and remember, too, their possible vulnerability.

Ideally, you should try to return papers relatively quickly: within a week or so of the due date. That reinforces your own insistence on imposing firm deadlines and penalties for lateness. More important, it maximizes the impact of your comments because students receive them while interest in the assignment remains high. A long delay often diminishes the value of your critique, because by then the students' attention has shifted to other matters. But teachers' schedules are not always easily controlled, and in the end it is more important to provide good comments than quick ones. If a reasonable delay in returning papers is the price of thorough evaluation, it is probably a price worth paying.

In evaluating any paper, it is important to have a clear idea of what you expect. Normally, you will probably evaluate a good research paper or essay on the basis of some or all of the following:

- *Thesis:* Is it clear or murky, derivative or original, persuasive or problematic?
- *Organization:* Does the paper flow in a logical, coherent manner?
- *Argument:* Is it persuasive, with the main points well supported with aptly chosen evidence from respectable sources? Is it balanced, with appropriate attention given to both positive points and possible objections?
- *Research:* Has the student identified proper sources, used them effectively, and done an acceptable amount of research based on your standards?
- *Prose style:* Is the writing lucid, error free, even graceful? Are there major problems of style, syntax, spelling?
- *Creativity:* Has the student, within the bounds of the assignment, shown unusual creativity in the selection and/or treatment of the subject? Has the creativity enhanced the assignment?

How you weight these criteria in relation to one another is, of course, up to you, but make sure your students understand your priorities.

Remember above all that when you are grading papers, you are not evaluating students, you are evaluating their work. This means you should not unfairly penalize a student who has somehow irritated you nor unfairly reward a stu-

dent whom you may particularly like. Some instructors ensure that they do not know the identity of a paper's author
when grading the work. That may be more trouble than it's
worth. But the principle is sound, because it suggests how
difficult it often is to separate personal feelings from professional judgments.

Personal feelings are most likely to interfere if you are
tired or frustrated when grading work. If you begin to feel
on edge, take a break. Don't take your edginess out on the
next paper. You should be careful as well about the order in
which you read the papers. Be suspicious of your immediate
reaction to a paper that comes on the heels of a wonderful
or dreadful one. A good paper may suffer unfairly in comparison to a terrific one; conversely, a poor paper may benefit
unfairly in comparison to a horrible one. If you find papers
that trouble you in some way, or about which you are truly
uncertain, keep them in a separate pile and return to them
when you have read all the others. That way you will have
a better perspective on the quality of the products of all your
students and will be more likely to have a clearer sense of
how to evaluate the problem cases.

The most important part of grading essays is writing
comments, which should be a blend of compliments, criticisms, and suggestions for improvement. Even the most disappointing paper should receive at least some positive comment. In fact, it is in some ways more important to reinforce
the author of a paper about which you have extensive criticisms than one that you consider nearly flawless. Find something positive about a paper, even if your principal reaction
is highly negative, and lead your comments with the best
thing you can say about it before turning to the problems.

With criticisms, be direct and relatively sparing. Don't
cover the pages in red ink. You can easily overwhelm students and may cause them to discard important comments
along with minor ones. Above all, let students know that criticism reflects not contempt but confidence in them, that it

shows how seriously you take their work and their potential for progress. Never be sarcastic or derisive or dismissive. If you make suggestions for revision, limit yourself to a few of the most important—and ask the student to concentrate on those. No one can concentrate on improving ten things at once, whether in baseball, music, or writing. So don't try to make them. Finally, always try to end on a positive note. It will leave students in a more receptive mood to consider your other comments.

If time and circumstances permit, it is a good idea to type your comments. For many people, that is a great deal faster than writing. It also ensures that the comments are legible and, if you are using a computer, that you will retain a copy of them for future reference. If you are grading a great many papers and your comments must of necessity be relatively brief, it may be easier to write them by hand on the essay itself. If so, be sure they are legible—and keep some record of your reaction in case students later have questions (or ask you for a letter of recommendation).

However careful you are in evaluating papers, there is almost always going to be disagreement over the results. You should not discourage students from challenging you on your reaction to their papers, but you should take a few steps to be sure their reactions are thoughtful ones. Ask students to wait at least a day before bringing a paper to you with questions or complaints. If the complaint sounds reasonable, offer to reread the paper—but reserve the right to lower as well as raise the grade. That will keep students from frivolously requesting a reread.

OPPORTUNITIES FOR REVISION

Under some circumstances, you may choose to offer your students the opportunity to revise their papers after they have submitted them. In general, the more important the paper—the greater the investment a student has in it—the stronger the case for allowing revisions. A chance to revise gives students the opportunity to benefit from, and respond to, criticisms from you or from their peers. And it makes more likely the creation of the best paper they can write.

If you do permit revisions, you should, of course, make that option available to everyone, not just to people whose papers are disappointing. Ideally, you should make clear at the start that students will have a second chance when papers are returned. Encourage (or require) students who plan to revise to meet with you first to discuss their papers. Give them a firm deadline. And of course be as clear as possible in explaining what revisions would be most helpful. In grading a revised paper, there is no need to repeat comments you have made on earlier drafts. Comment instead on whatever improvements there have been and on what problems may still remain.

Permitting revisions is not always possible, or even desirable. The biggest problem is scheduling. Papers due near the end of the term seldom come in early enough to allow time for revisions. In a course with multiple papers, revisions are often impractical for both the students and the instructor. Another problem is that if students know they will have a chance to revise, they may not devote as much effort to a first draft as they would otherwise. Under any circumstances, revising papers creates more work for your students and for you. Be sure you, and they, have time to devote to this extra effort before you encourage them to make it.

SHARING STUDENT RESEARCH

Research papers and serious critical essays are the most original things most students do in academia. Scholars undertake such projects in the expectation that other people will read them. There is considerable value in encouraging your students to do the same; so it is worth considering ways to make your students' work available to the entire class—and even to people outside the class.

The simplest way to allow students to share their work is through an informal activity, such as an unstructured discussion. In the course of the term, you might choose from time to time to steer discussions toward topics on which your students are working and ask the appropriate students to report on their research or other work. You might also set aside a class, or several classes, in which students will be asked to give short reports on their work—perhaps including examples of their research or samples of the texts they are examining. Be sure, however, to give them strict time limits and to enforce them. Peer review panels provide another effective way for students to present their research and learn what their classmates have discovered. Panels can be composed of several students working on related topics. They will present brief summaries of their work to the class, and then comment on one another's work. Other members of the class can, of course, join in the discussion. Web pages are another alternative (see chapter 10). If you have already established a page for your class, you can give students a chance to post their papers, or abstracts of their papers, and then assign them to the rest of the class as optional or mandatory reading.

There are, of course, many other ways in which student work can become available to others. By making individual discoveries available to the whole class—as well as to the intellectual community beyond—you treat your students as scholars and give them a greater stake in their work. You also broaden the amount of information and number of viewpoints to which they are exposed.

Doing research and writing papers is, in many disciplines, the most important and most challenging form of learning. Students take much more pride in work they have created themselves than they do in any other kind of work. They also discover a form of learning that no classroom experience can replicate. It may not always be possible to incorporate research and writing into your courses. But when it is possible, make an effort to do so and emphasize its importance. There are great potential rewards in giving students the experience of creation.

SIX

TESTING AND EVALUATION

Tests and examinations are not usually a student's, or a teacher's, favorite exercise. But they need not be traumatic or disillusioning. Fair tests, thoughtfully constructed, can be not just a valuable tool of evaluation but also a tool for learning. Preparing examinations, and preparing your students for examinations, is an important part of most courses.

It is, of course, not always necessary to give tests or exams. Some courses use papers or projects as the basis for evaluation instead. That has the advantage of directing the attention of students to their writing and their independent work. It has the disadvantage of providing you with no opportunity to evaluate how well they have mastered the basic ideas and skills you have been trying to teach them—and of providing them with less incentive to do so.

In most cases, however, some kind of exam will be appropriate. And in many cases, it may be required by your institution, whether you like it or not. It is, therefore, important to know how to design exams that are effective, fair, challenging, and creative. The goal is to construct tests that give students a chance to show what they know—not what they don't; that cover a range of material or skills so that all students have a reasonably equal chance of success (not just those that have mastered one particular skill or body of knowledge); and that force students to think rather than merely recite facts.

There are both strategic and tactical issues lurking behind the creation and implementation of every test, from the simple surprise quiz to the elaborate final exam. The time to think about these matters is not a few days or even weeks before you plan to give the exam. The time to do it is before the course begins. That way you can decide how to relate the material you cover in your course with the expectations you will have of your students when the time comes for tests. Needless to say, you should not—to use a term often associated with secondary school preoccupation with college entrance examinations—"teach to the test," although in this case, of course, any test to which you teach will be one of your own devising. But it does make sense to consider exams an integral part of your course and to give them the same amount of consideration that you would to choosing a reading list, designing activities, or preparing lectures.

KEEPING STUDENTS INFORMED ABOUT TESTS

Whatever kinds of tests you give, make sure your students are fully informed about them. Announce the dates of exams well in advance. Remember that like you, students have busy lives and need to plan their schedules. Do not reschedule an exam casually. In the face of a "vocal minority" who may want a change, a "silent majority" may expect you to hold firm. Before you decide to change your schedule, make sure that it will serve all—or at least most—of your students, and that it will not be too disruptive to you.

Provide complete information well in advance about the content and format of any exam. The goal of a test is to reinforce skills and to find out what students know—not to catch them by surprise. Give them a rough sense of how much the exam will draw on readings, lectures, discussions, or research. Making old tests available to all students will help them visualize the format, force you to rework previous efforts, and eliminate the possibility that some clever individuals might gain an advantage through access to "bootleg" copies. (Sometimes, of course, there is good reason to use questions from old exams again, so think carefully about whether you plan to do that before releasing copies to your students. If you do plan to draw from old exams, however, it is better to draw from tests several years old, not from ones that students currently on campus may have taken.) Above all, early disclosure will force you to think about the exam in advance and avoid writing it in a rush the night before.

Make the value of the test clear. If it will constitute a large proportion of the students' final grades, stress the fact and create conditions that will help them prepare for it—such as review sessions or a reduced reading load around the time of the test. If it is worth relatively little, make sure that students keep their eyes open to other, more important, evaluations down the road.

PLANNING FOR EXAMINATIONS

One of the first things to decide is how many tests you plan to give, and when you plan to give them. The appropriate decision on this issue will vary tremendously, depending on where you teach, whom you teach, how you teach, and what you teach. What is important is that your testing strategy and your teaching strategy are compatible. Frequent tests or quizzes often help weaker students master manageable amounts of material. They also allow you to monitor the progress, comprehension, and effort of the students—particularly if you suspect it has flagged when it comes to doing the assignments. But they consume precious class time as well as student and teacher energy.

The most common pattern of testing in colleges and universities is the traditional model of a midterm and a final. In some places, it may also be the mandatory pattern. That model has many advantages. It requires minimal class time. It forces students to synthesize large amounts of material. And it allows you to use the exams to turn your attention—and theirs—to broad themes and ideas. One drawback is that it offers only one opportunity for students to respond to evaluation before the course comes to an end. Another is that many students have difficulty absorbing large amounts of material. A possible compromise is to begin with relatively frequent evaluations and gradually extend the period between them. This is easier if you are teaching a year-long rather than a single-term course.

But exams are not only a factor in students' lives. They are a factor in yours. Unless you have a large course with teaching assistants, you will be the one both to write and to grade the examinations, and you should think carefully about your own schedule and responsibilities. Do not create impossible burdens for yourself. If you do, both you and your students will be shortchanged.

In addition to deciding how many exams to give, you will need to decide when to give them. In some cases your department will make the decision for you by establishing times when you must test so as to not conflict with other courses. But if the decision is yours, keep several things in mind:

If possible, choose dates that reflect natural breaks in the material you are covering. You should also choose dates that do not conflict with, or come too near to, other likely student obligations in your course and outside it. You should be aware of dates of schoolwide importance (such as major athletic or social events) as well as those of countrywide importance (such as tests like the LSAT, MCAT, GRE, etc.). You should also consider other courses that the students are likely to take and when they will have exams. And, again, do not forget about yourself. Since you are probably teaching several courses, it is a good idea to stagger your workload as much as possible, especially since you may want (or have) to evaluate the exams rapidly.

You need to think as well about where the students will take the exams—in class, or at home. Each has advantages and disadvantages. An in-class exam forces students to master the material so that they are prepared to present it rapidly under the artificial constraint of time pressure. It tends to reward those who have prepared carefully, who react well to pressure, who form their thoughts quickly and write rapidly, and who know how to anticipate the questions you will ask. It tends to penalize those who have spent less time preparing or who take longer to formulate or write answers.

A take-home exam, by contrast, permits students to write their essays under a less artificial constraint, such as a twenty-four- or forty-eight-hour deadline. It allows them to think more carefully about the questions you ask them, to pay more attention to organization and writing, and—if you permit it (as you probably should, since you will have no way to enforce a prohibition)—to consult sources. A take-home exam becomes less a test of memory and more a test of thinking and writing. There are also benefits to you: You will receive typed answers and will not have to worry about deciphering your students' handwriting, which is often at its worst on hastily written exams. And it will allow you to apply regular standards of organization, grammar, evidence, and thought. There are also significant drawbacks. Students will be tempted to spend less time preparing, thinking that they can retrieve the information they need during the day or so they have to write the exam. Some students may receive unauthorized help, something it will be very difficult for you to monitor. Finally, most students will certainly write longer essays than they would in class.

It is, of course, possible to combine the two approaches, with an in-class component that includes relatively specific questions designed to test students' knowledge of the material you have presented to them, and a take-home component that includes longer essays or problems that will test their ability to frame and support arguments. Another compromise is to distribute a group of exam questions in advance, while informing your students that only one or two of them will appear on the exam. Students will then have to prepare broadly, but will not have to prepare indiscriminately.

PREPARING STUDENTS FOR EXAMS

In many cases, teachers assume that because students have taken tests before, they need no preparation to take them now. But all exams are different. Students who have taken multiple-choice or standardized tests for many years may have no idea how to write an essay on an examination. If you are concerned about how well your students are prepared, survey the class well in advance of the first exam to see what experiences they have had; or give them an assignment that will allow you to determine how well prepared your students actually are for the kind of exam you will be giving them. You might choose to use part of a class period to offer some practical tips on how to write a timed essay—perhaps by giving them a sample question and asking them, either individually or in groups, to outline a response. Whatever else you do, emphasize to them that they should always think first (even if for only a few minutes) and organize their thoughts before actually writing their essays. Another way to help students prepare for exams, and to make the process less intimidating, is to provide models of successful essays or good responses to short-answer questions so that students can see clearly what you expect.

The last step in preparing students for the exam is to use the test itself to guide them into their work. Always include written directions on your exam, particularly mechanical requirements such as how many questions students should answer, how they should label their essays, how much time they should devote to each section. Your instructions should not be too long; you will not want your students to use a lot of valuable time reading directions. But they should be full enough to ensure that students know what is expected of them.

HANDLING MISSED EXAMINATIONS

It is inevitable that from time to time students will fail to take, or be unable to take, your examinations. Illness, family emergencies, oversleeping, schedule conflicts, and a host of other reasons—good and bad—will leave you with the task of deciding how, and whether, to allow students to make up for their absences.

On this issue, your department or your school may have policies that will determine your options. Make sure you know the rules. To whatever degree you are permitted to establish your own policy, try to produce one that does not reward those who miss exams out of negligence or penalize those who have legitimate reasons for their absence. Keep the following rules in mind:

- Insist that students who anticipate an unavoidable conflict inform you at least a day or two ahead of the exam.
- If you plan to give a makeup exam, establish the date in advance. Make it as soon as possible after the original exam so that students do not forget the material or learn too much about the original exam. Choose a time that will not con-

flict with other courses (and perhaps one that will require a certain amount of inconvenience, to discourage students from choosing this option)—an early morning, evening, even (if it is possible at your institution) a Saturday.

- Revise the original exam with care. Replace multiple-choice or short-answer questions that will obviously leak to absent members of the class. But do not necessarily discard an essay question that is well constructed and addresses a major theme of your course. Instead, change the wording somewhat or reformulate it with a slightly different slant.

- If you have distributed a group of essay questions in advance from which you were planning to select one or two for the exam, choose some of the unused questions for the makeup.

CONSTRUCTING AN EXAM

The most important task in examining students is constructing the examination itself. The goal of an exam is to evaluate how well students have learned the themes, skills, and content you consider important and that you emphasized in your course—not to trick or "catch" them. Examinations can consist of several different kinds of questions in many different combinations.

The *essay question* is the most challenging and in many ways the most valuable kind for students in most fields in the social sciences and humanities. There is truly no substitute if you want your students to engage in higher-level thinking. A good essay question will not stress memorization of facts. It will instead take a significant theme from your course and ask students to develop their own interpretation or response using information that they have encountered in class and in the readings. It should also provide them with both structure and room for initiative. Finally, it should produce a range of responses that reflects the varied abilities and perspectives of your students. Use verbs like "analyze," "assess," "compare," "contrast," "discuss," "explain," and "evaluate" to signal an open-ended, higher-order question. Avoid verbs like "list" or "describe" that will generate responses with little analysis, unless you intend to use them in conjunction with those that require critical thought. Choose questions that are neither too broad nor too specific. Be sure students can answer them in the time allotted. Steer clear of multipart questions unless you clearly identify each component.

Among the most familiar kinds of essay questions are ones that ask students to respond to a statement or passage of text. You might present them with a quotation from another scholar, or from a primary source, and ask them to respond to the claims the author has made. You can also make up a quotation of your own and ask them to respond to it. But make sure that any quotation raises a question clearly and unambiguously. A good essay question should not require arduous deciphering.

You might also consider giving your students primary source documents to analyze and integrate with their answer to a question. Ask how the documents shed light on the question. The addition of document analysis will reinforce critical thought, give weaker students a prop or two for their essay, and provide stronger students with the opportunity to generate more sophisticated syntheses.

Reread the questions after you have written them. Ask yourself if the language is too broad or vague, or subject to interpretations you do not intend. If you are at all uncertain about them, ask colleagues if it seems to "work." If you are teaching a course with teaching assistants, give them a chance to react to the questions; they, after all, will be grading at least some of the responses to them, and they are, after you, the people most familiar with the material in your course. If you are a teaching assistant yourself who has been asked to draft exam questions, confer with your fellow teaching assistants.

The *multiple-choice question* has a bad reputation. Many consider it a crutch for lazy teachers or lazy students, who want to focus only on rote memorization. But multiple-choice questions, when crafted with care, can test the ability of students to apply analogies, synthesize interpretations, analyze texts, and sequence events. When used in conjunction with essay or short-answer questions, they can help provide broad and balanced coverage of the course content. They can also add an objective component to your test, highlight possible flaws in your teaching, and give poor writers a chance to improve their grades.

A multiple-choice question consists of a *stem* (the body of the question before the choices are presented), the incorrect responses (sometimes known as *distractors*), and the correct answer (known as the *key*). Use clear language in the stem. Avoid double negatives and obscure terminology. Emphasize important ideas, events, or individuals, not trivia. Use the same number of responses in any group of questions; five is the norm. Make the responses similar in format, length, and grammar; do not introduce unnecessary complications for students. Avoid "all of the above" or "none of the above" responses unless it seems absolutely necessary or appropriate. Last but not least, proofread carefully to be certain that the question makes sense and has only one right answer.

Some instructors design multiple-choice tests so that the most difficult questions come at the end of the test. This helps reduce the likelihood of students' panicking early on when confronted with a question they cannot answer. It also means that slow readers will have a better chance of getting through the test without getting hung up on hard questions at the start.

The *short-answer question* is a good compromise between the essay and the multiple-choice question. It allows you to test for factual knowledge and critical thought without placing hefty writing burdens on the students or onerous grading burdens on yourself, and it is less limiting than a multiple-choice question. Ideally, it should be used in combination with other types of questions to create a broad and balanced exam. There are several types of short-answer questions:

- *Identifications* typically require that students provide a brief synopsis (a few sentences) of a person, event, or term. Insist that they also describe why the person or event or idea is significant and that they relate their description to a theme of the course.

- *Clusters* consist of lists of ideas, items, or events. Students are asked to place the material in the proper order and explain why the sequence makes sense. Or you can provide a list of terms and have students put them in pairs and explain the relationship between the elements in each pair.

- *Source-based questions* can be particularly useful in terms of skill development. Present students with a written (chart, graph, cartoon, or document), visual (video clip, slide, or photograph), or audio (music or other recording) source; ask students briefly to identify whichever of the following are appropriate to the source: the author, intended audience, relation to larger themes, and point of view.

AVOIDING CHEATING ON TESTS

Just as you must be alert to the possibility of plagiarism in written assignments, you need to be alert to the possibility of cheating on tests. Most students are honest, but there will often be some who will be tempted to act improperly in taking tests—out of cunning, fear, or weakness. There are some steps you can take to make cheating more difficult.

Certain kinds of questions, such as multiple choice, are easy targets for cheating; students can easily look at the work of others while taking the exam. Even on essay exams, students might bring crib sheets into class or arrive with material already written in blue books. You can help prevent this kind of cheating by giving two different sets of multiple-choice questions, randomly distributed among students, and of course by actively monitoring exams—and making sure students know you are doing so—to discourage wandering eyes. To avoid situations where students try to substitute blue books in which they have written in advance for the ones you distribute, keep close track of blue books during the term and try to make sure that blank ones do not circulate. Also, avoid repeating essay questions from one year to the next.

GRADING TESTS

Once you have created and administered the test, you will have to grade it. Do not procrastinate. The task will not become easier if you delay. And if you wait too long to grade tests given before the term ends, the opportunity to use the test as a learning instrument will disappear as both you and the students move on to new subjects and concerns. So try to return the test as soon as you can, within a week if possible.

Establishing a set of standards or criteria for essays before you begin will help you to grade quickly and fairly. It will also help students understand why they received the grade they did since you may not have the time or inclination to write extensive comments on their exams. Some typical criteria for essay questions include the following: Does the essay contain a clear and well-developed *thesis* that answers the question directly? Does the essay demonstrate critical and/or original *analysis* or *thought*? Does the essay support its thesis and analysis with substantial and relevant *evidence* from appropriate sources? Is the *style* of the essay appropriate? Is it well organized and well written given the time pressures? Is the essay marred by major *errors* that detract substantially from the argument?

There is no one right way to grade an exam. You might choose to break the exam into its component parts and grade each separately—for example, do multiple-choice sections for all students first, followed by short-answer and essay sections. Skim several exams so that you can get a feel for what an average paper looks like and what grades are appropriate for what level of performance. Try to grade comparable essays in a group. That is, if students had a choice between questions A and B, first evaluate all of the A exams and then all the B exams. Write the grades in pencil at first or keep them on a separate sheet of paper so that you can change them if necessary. Sometimes an essay will, on an initial reading, appear inordinately good or bad in comparison to what has come just before it; your evaluation may change after you have read more. Give yourself frequent breaks so that your mood does not affect your scores.

Consider evaluating the overall quality of the exam at the end, reflecting on the grades you assigned to the separate sections. You may wish to alter the subjective grades slightly in order to give each student the overall grade you think he or she deserves.

If time allows—and often it will not—write comments on your exams, but not extensive ones. For essays, make concise references to the criteria or standards you set. For short-answer or multiple-choice questions, simply indicate what the correct answer is if the student has made an error. A general principle for providing comments is to write enough so that if a student brings you the exam later and asks you to explain the grade, reading your own comments will remind you of why you evaluated it as you did. As with commenting on papers, you should be careful to comment on exams respectfully and, as much as possible, encouragingly. Do not spare students criticism when they have made mistakes or done poorly; but try to include some encouragement or praise if there is any basis for it. And never write comments that will seem condescending, scornful, or nasty. Write as if the students you are grading are doing their best, even if you suspect that is not the case.

Although exams that come in the midst of the term should be returned quickly, they should not leave your possession until you have had a chance to reflect on what the exam has told you about your students' learning. When you do return the exam, spend some time in class discussing any problems or trends you have diagnosed. It often helps to distribute an especially good answer to a question (with the student's permission, and preferably anonymously) and lead a discussion of why it was so successful. But there are dangers to this approach. If your model essay is dramatically better than the norm, there is a danger that it will intimidate some students; if it is not, it may annoy students who think their essays were equally good or even better. You can avoid some of these dangers by preparing and distributing a model essay you have written yourself, although the problem of possible intimidation may be even greater in that case.

Keep grades confidential. Do not leave graded papers out in the open for students to retrieve, since that will give students a chance to see other students' grades. (It may also tempt students to steal good papers by others for future use.) Many states have laws maintaining confidentiality of student records and a student's right to privacy, and most universities have codes of their own. But whatever the rules of your institution, grades are never issues to discuss with anyone but the student involved.

Remember, finally, that the fault for a disappointing performance on your exam may lie neither in your students nor in the stars but in the exam or the class itself. Reread your questions carefully after you have graded the exams and ask yourself whether the way you constructed your questions was responsible for the problems your students had. If there were consistent gaps in students' knowledge or skills, the chances are that either the exam was faulty or there was something wrong with the way you presented the material or taught the skills in your course. Reevaluating what succeeded and failed previously is a vital part of constructing and reconstructing exams. It is also a vital part of helping you evaluate your own teaching.

Even the most gifted and experienced teachers can benefit from evaluations of their performance. Feedback from students or colleagues can alert you to aspects of your classroom behavior, small or large, that might be distracting, irritating, or confusing to those you teach. Careful self-evaluation can also help you recognize weaknesses you might not have noticed if you had not spent the time looking for them.

FORMS OF EVALUATION

In many, perhaps most, schools, you will have very little control over some forms of evaluation. Evaluations are often required by institutions—and sometimes even by law—and are one of the ways teachers are monitored by their employers. Such evaluations may become a permanent part of faculty personnel files and can have an impact on salaries and promotions. Institutions often require teachers to use standardized evaluation forms which may not be altered, although it is sometimes permissible to attach additional questions pertaining to a specific course. A formal evaluation typically comes at or near the end of a course.

But it is usually possible for teachers to organize informal evaluations on their own, whatever the institution requires. Such evaluations can come at any point in the term and can ask for an overall assessment of the course or of one discrete aspect of it. To get informal feedback quickly, you might ask students to answer a question or two about some aspect of the class on note cards and return them to you at the end of class. A "spot" evaluation of that sort might ask students to tell you whether they understood the main points of a lecture or discussion; whether they found the required readings useful; or whether they saw the significance of a particular learning activity. For a broader assessment of your teaching, and of the course as a whole, you might construct a midterm evaluation, which could allow you to make changes before the end of the course.

CONSTRUCTING EVALUATIONS

If you do have any control over the form in which students are asked to evaluate your teaching, you should keep in mind some simple guidelines for constructing questions that will elicit useful responses. There are a number of different kinds of questions you can ask, each of which will elicit different kinds of responses. Some questions ask students to write out a response in their own words; others ask them to use a numerical scale to evaluate aspects of the course or the instructor. Evaluations often combine several types of questions.

If you are presenting your students with open-ended questions, be careful not to make them *too* open-ended. If you ask a single question such as "What do you think of this class?" you will likely get a range of responses that comment on everything from the assigned reading to the subject matter to your clothing choices. You will also probably get a lot of generalizations ("a great course") and a few irrelevant remarks ("I hated getting up at eight o'clock to make this lecture"). To avoid this problem, construct evaluations, particularly longer ones used at the end of courses, that ask students to comment on specific parts of the course and specific aspects of your teaching abilities. For example, ask about lecturing techniques, required reading, classroom atmosphere, availability of the instructor, use of multimedia material, or whatever other specific issues are relevant to your course.

It is usually best to have a mix of questions, some of which require written responses and some of which require ranking on a numbered scale. The former will give you a more textured response to your teaching, the latter a more statistically reliable one. Finally, arrange the questions into groups. One group of questions might ask students about your lectures, another about discussion sections or labs, another about assignments, another about collaborative exercises or independent projects.

ADMINISTERING
EVALUATIONS

Written course evaluations demand rigorous administration if you want students to take them seriously. Explain to the students why you are doing an evaluation and how you will use the results. Make it clear that their evaluations will have no bearing on their grades in the course. Give them enough time to answer all of the questions and thank them for doing it. Keep all student evaluations anonymous and leave the room while the students are completing them. Ask student volunteers to collect the evaluations, put them in an envelope, and deliver them to your department or your mailbox. If instructors collect the evaluations themselves, students will be rightly concerned that they might lose their anonymity. Some schools require that evaluations conducted at the end of the class be sealed and not returned to the teacher until final grades have been registered; you might consider assuring students that you and your coinstructors will not read the evaluations until after the grades are in even if there is no rule requiring you to do so. Otherwise, students may be concerned that something they write will give away their identity and affect your evaluation of their work.

USING INTERMEDIARIES FOR EVALUATIONS

If you want a more probing evaluation, in which students are prodded to discuss your teaching in ways that a written form will not encourage them to do, you may wish to involve an intermediary. Students will naturally be very reluctant to discuss with you directly their honest reactions to your teaching. You might consider arranging for them to have a conversation about your course with a neutral third party. If your institution employs teaching consultants (as some do), ask a consultant to come into your class for a few minutes toward the end of a period and interview your students after you have left. You should discuss with the consultant in advance the questions you would like students to consider. If the class is small, for example a seminar with ten to twelve students, such a discussion can take place with the entire group. Larger classes might break into smaller groups, discuss the questions among themselves, and then make group reports to the interviewer. The interviewer might take notes, summarize them for the class, ask for clarification, and then write up the results or discuss them with you. Alternatively, you might wish the interviewer to give you the raw data of a classroom observation, rather than distilling it, if you fear student reactions might not be properly interpreted by an outsider. While this method might take more class time than you are willing to give, it does provide a way for students to discuss their views without having to confront you directly.

If a consultant is not available, or if you prefer not to use one, another way to involve intermediaries in the evaluation process is to call on your own colleagues—fellow teachers who are themselves wrestling with many of the same problems and questions you are. The simplest way to get help from colleagues in the evaluation process is to solicit their comments on your syllabi, papers, readings, and exams. A disinterested critic can often pick up on elements of your course materials—their tone, the overall impression they give—that might escape you. Such simple assessments often lead naturally to an exchange of ideas on teaching resources and techniques, which is often one of the most enjoyable parts of professional life.

Once you have established a relationship with some of your colleagues that makes peer evaluation comfortable for all of you, you might ask some of them to visit your classroom from time to time and offer some advice. If you ask a peer to visit your class, give some thought to how to make it a productive assessment experience. Wait until you feel comfortable with the group of students before you ask an outsider to visit. The students will by then be focused less on the guest than on the class. Pick a typical classroom activity, rather than something unusual that you are trying for the first time. If possible, be sure there is student interaction or initiative rather than straight lecturing.

You will likely be somewhat nervous if a colleague is visiting your class. Try to reduce your anxiety by ensuring that you know exactly when the visitor is coming and by familiarizing your colleague with what the students are doing and how it fits into the larger aims of the course. If there are specific characteristics of your teaching on which you would like reactions or advice, alert your evaluator to them. And tell your students in advance that a visitor will sit in on a class. Do not surprise or confuse them by inserting a stranger into the room without notice.

Have a follow-up discussion with the evaluator as soon

as possible after the visit rather than waiting until the class has faded from memory. If you want a written evaluation for your own records or your professional file, ask the visitor to compose one. You might also arrange for another visit later in the course to get an idea of how you are improving.

Relationships among colleagues are different in every institution, and this kind of consultation may not seem appropriate in many cases. If you are an untenured member of a department, you may be reluctant to expose yourself to the scrutiny of more senior members, particularly if you do not know them very well. Even if there are no hierarchical issues, you may well feel uncomfortable interacting with your colleagues in this way—and you may have good reason to do so. But if you have a sufficiently secure and comfortable relationship with colleagues, it is often to your benefit to ask for their help.

LEARNING FROM OTHER TEACHERS

We all learn, to some extent, by imitation. Recall the teachers who most excited or inspired you. What was it about them that made their classes such memorable experiences? How did they spark your interest or push you to read the extra book or write the most difficult paper with success? You should never discount your own experience on the other side of the desk as you try to figure out what makes a good class or great teacher.

When you think about courses you have taken yourself, consider particularly those most similar to the ones you are teaching now. What worked and what didn't? Why? How was the class structured and conducted? Make a list of particularly useful assignments or reading materials. What lecture and discussion techniques were especially appealing? How were audiovisual materials employed? Were there any unusual teaching methods that were effective? Evaluate your own class experiences and use the information to benefit your teaching.

You need not rely solely on your memories of your own experience as a student. Your fellow teachers can also provide inspiration and examples. One of the best ways to evaluate your own teaching is to watch others teach and try to decide what you can learn from them. So it is worth considering visiting the classes of fellow teachers, especially the classes of teachers you admire or whose reputations as teachers are good. If you are having trouble keeping your students awake during your lectures, sit in on a class of a celebrated lecturer in your department. If discussions seem to end long before they should, visit a seminar that has a reputation of being persistently lively.

The feasibility of visiting other instructors' classes (like the feasibility of having other teachers visit yours) will depend, of course, on the culture of your school or department—and your relationship with the teachers in question. You should never attend another teacher's class without asking permission in advance, and you should only ask permission if you feel certain that the request will not seem intrusive or inappropriate. If you do ask to visit a colleague's class, make clear that it is because you are aware of his or her reputation as an excellent teacher and think you might learn something from the experience.

If actually visiting classes is not possible or comfortable, you can learn a great deal from your colleagues simply through conversation—talking with them about how they teach, what assignments they use, which techniques work for them and which don't. Everyone around you wrestles each day with the same problems you do, and one way or another you should make them into a resource for your own teaching.

You can learn from other teachers, but of course you cannot become them. When observing or talking with others, distinguish between techniques and approaches that you yourself might find useful and those with which you would feel uncomfortable. Teaching is a very personal act, and what works for one instructor may not be compatible with the personality of another. But when you see a successful teaching technique that appears foreign to you, do not dismiss it too quickly. Experiment with different approaches; use those that work for you and discard those that do not. Through trial and error and repeated practice in the classroom, you will define your own style. But shop around before you choose the teaching techniques most suited for you.

Remember, finally, that times—and students—change. What works now may not work at all in ten years, with a new generation of students. Some effective teaching methods are timeless, but others need to be adjusted as styles and customs change.

ASSESSING YOURSELF ON VIDEOTAPE

Some schools provide facilities that make it possible for you to videotape your classes and then review your performance, either on your own or with the help of teaching consultants. Even if your school does not provide such facilities, you can probably arrange to tape a class yourself with a simple home video camera. Instructors often find this a particularly valuable exercise, even if sometimes a difficult one.

Seeing yourself on camera in front of a class can be a humbling experience. Most of us have idealized views of what we look and sound like, and seeing ourselves as we appear to others can sometimes come as a shock. Few of us care to know how many times we say "uh" or "you know" in a fifty-minute period. But remember that what might look or sound strange to you is probably not at all strange to your students, who have always known you as you are now discovering yourself. Remember, too, that a videotape of a discussion or lecture is the "truest" representation of your teaching. In fact, in some ways it is less obtrusive than a visitor, particularly if the camera operates itself without a visiting techician. In a sense, it allows you to visit your own classroom. Once you get over the shock of seeing yourself through the camera's eye, there is much you can learn from the experience.

Some institutions have media services that can arrange for you to videotape your class. A campus teaching center, if you have one, can usually help you evaluate the results. It is often useful to watch the videotape with a trained evaluator, an experienced teacher, or a small group of colleagues. It may make you uneasy to view yourself in the presence of others, but your own reaction is likely to be so colored by the uncomfortable novelty of seeing yourself on film that getting more impartial reactions from others can be of great value. Whether you watch the tape by yourself or with others, evaluate it with specific written criteria, which might include interaction with students, organization, clarity of presentation, questioning techniques, classroom atmosphere, voice, and body movement.

As with other evaluations, tell the students ahead of time what will happen and pick a typical class. If you are handling the taping yourself, be sure the camera is at an angle that will permit a view of both you and your students. If possible, use two cameras, one focused on you and one on the students so that you can see what they are doing as you teach and how they are reacting to you. If you think taping is useful, try to tape more than one class during the term. Schedule a session in the fifth or sixth week of class so you will have enough time to evaluate the tape and act on suggestions for improvement, and then tape at least once more during the course to measure your progress. One advantage of videotape is that you can keep a record of your teaching to chart improvement.

Of course both you and your students may well feel self-conscious under the gaze of a camera, at least at first. Be prepared for some unusual dynamics at the beginning. After a while, however, most people get used to the presence of the camera and even forget about it—and it is these later moments in the class that you should evaluate most carefully.

RESPONDING TO EVALUATIONS

You would be well advised to take advantage of some, perhaps many, of the various evaluation methods available to you. But you also need to be careful in dealing with the results. As hard as it may be, try to separate the professional from the personal. Evaluations, from whatever source, are (or at least should be) responses to your professional abilities, not your personal qualities. Even if students make rude comments about your appearance or behavior or personality, keep in mind that the only basis for such comments is your performance in the classroom. The students know your teaching; they usually do not know you.

Try to remind yourself that you cannot be all things to all people. You will usually have some students who do not like the way you teach or the subject matter you present but find themselves in your course anyway. The larger the course, the more malcontents you are likely to encounter. Many instructors are tempted to ignore the positive evaluations of their performance, even if such evaluations are the vast majority of the total, and remember only the critical comments. If several students in a large lecture class say your lectures are dull while most of the others find them lively, look at the numbers. On the other hand, don't ignore criticisms that crop up repeatedly in evaluations. Look for recurring comments in student evaluations rather than the isolated reaction. One glowing response in a set of mediocre reactions should not leave you satisfied any more than one negative evaluation in the midst of positive ones should leave you distressed.

If evaluations come in the middle of the term, separate

the criticisms into various categories. Look for ones that you can act on immediately. Identify those that you might consider using as the basis of change in future courses. On some points, you might let the students know that you are modifying classroom activities or your teaching style as a result of suggestions they made that you found helpful. That can give them a stronger sense of participation in the learning process, of being to some degree partners in your common effort. But there will likely be some aspects of your course that you will decide not to change regardless of criticism.

Identify problems with which you need outside help. While it is tempting to think you can solve all your teaching difficulties on your own, you may reach a point where your frustration and exasperation will need an outlet. If you're having a chronic problem that defies solution, with a class, an individual student, or any aspect of teaching, seek assistance—from a colleague, from a teaching center, from friends or family members who may know you well enough to have suggestions that would not occur to professional associates. Articulating your frustrations often helps you to clarify the problems, get constructive feedback, and collaborate on ways to improve your situation. It also helps to talk it out and realize that you are not the only instructor who has faced difficulties.

Realize that you can be both a good scholar *and* a good teacher. The two are not mutually exclusive. Being a good teacher does not mean that you are not a "real scholar." Great research scholars are often effective instructors. A truly successful academic life draws strength from both teaching and research.

FINDING CAMPUS TEACHING RESOURCES

There are usually many resources in schools, colleges, and universities that can help you improve your teaching, some of which may not appear immediately useful for that purpose. The obvious place to start for any beginning instructor is in your own department, which can give you information about teaching conventions and traditions in your field. Your department might also provide sample syllabi, equipment, a specialized library, an audiovisual collection, and, of course, the expertise of its members. See if your department sponsors teaching workshops or an evaluation program.

Many campuses have teaching centers specifically intended for new instructors. Staffed by professionals who offer a range of support activities, they often conduct ongoing teaching workshops, provide individual counseling, assist in creating evaluations, review videotapes of classes, and offer a library on teaching.

If you are a graduate student teacher, consult your department's or institution's graduate student organizations, which can be another valuable source for teaching handbooks, evaluations, workshops, and general information about teaching at a college or university. Because such organizations are usually staffed and run by graduate students, they have the advantage of giving you the view from the trenches rather than the headquarters.

While we don't usually think of the library as a place to improve our teaching, reference librarians trained in specific subject areas are an essential resource for anyone teaching a class with research as a component. They will familiarize you with collections, help to plan research assignments, and, most important, give specialized library tours. Some college libraries even offer term-paper services for both students and teachers. With advance warning of your research assignments, librarians can guide you and your students to resources you may not have known existed.

Student learning centers are designed to help students more than teachers. But because they tend to focus on study skills and writing deficiencies, they are in a good position to give you advice about structuring assignments. They are also places to which you can refer students who are having difficulties with the work in your class. If you have disabled students in your class, your institution likely has a support service that can arrange for note takers, signers, and alternative exam administration (for example, exams without time limits, oral exams, or exams taken on computer).

Campus media or audiovisual centers may be able to help you arrange videotaping and provide equipment for classroom use. Some maintain a lending library of videos, films, slides, and audiotapes. They may also teach you how to use the equipment or provide you with someone who can operate it for you.

A campus computer center is an obvious place to learn how to integrate computerized activities into your course or how to supplement classroom activities. It might also provide you with software to use in your teaching. Some offer courses on using computers for teaching.

The Internet can hook you into all sorts of teaching resources, including sample syllabi, departments' and professors' web pages, teaching centers at other institutions, publishing houses, bibliographies, government education initiatives at all levels, and many more. Your computer center may be able to help you identify appropriate web sites. Keep an eye out, too, for articles on teaching in professional newsletters, in the *Chronicle of Higher Education,* and in other publications which try to share teaching experiences broadly.

SAMPLE EVALUATIONS

Below are some sample evaluation forms designed for various purposes. Your own course will undoubtedly have special needs of its own, but you may wish to use one of the following forms as a starting point for your own.

For a graduate student leading a discussion section; to be administered during the first several weeks of class.

Please circle the number which is most appropriate and write answers to the other questions.

1. Do you find discussion sections helpful?
   Very helpful 7 6 5 4 3 2 1 Not helpful
2. What might be improved about the section?
3. How would you rate the instructor on the following?
   a. Approachability? 7 6 5 4 3 2 1
   b. As a facilitator of discussion? 7 6 5 4 3 2 1
   c. Knowledge of subject? 7 6 5 4 3 2 1
   d. As an evaluator of your work? 7 6 5 4 3 2 1
   e. What suggestions can you make for improvement of the items above?
4. Is there any topic or activity not presently included in the section which should be added? Why?
5. Is there any topic or activity that should be omitted? Why?
6. Feel free to make any additional comments about the class.

Thanks for taking the time to complete this form!

For an instructor during the first several weeks of the term.
Please answer the following questions concerning the course. Fill in the blank space with the appropriate number ranking from most effective to least effective. Do not write your name on this form.

Circle your student status:

Freshman Sophomore Junior Senior Graduate
Most Effective   Average   Least Effective
7   6   5   4   3   2   1

1. Are the course objectives clear? _____
2. Are the lectures clear and organized? _____
3. Is the reading useful? _____
4. Are discussions helpful? _____

5. Are the writing assignments useful? _____

6. Does the classroom atmosphere facilitate your learning? _____

7. Is the instructor accessible outside of the classroom? _____

Please evaluate each of the books we are reading: [List them.]

Comment on any aspect of the course, particularly lectures, required reading, and writing assignments, and offer suggestions on how the course might be improved. Thank you for your time.

For an instructor at the end of a course. These are sample questions that might be used to elicit narrative responses, or they could be adapted for a quantitative rating.

Evaluate yourself as a student in this course.

1. How much effort and preparation did you put into each class?

2. What do you think is your role as a student in the course?

Evaluate the performance of the instructor.

1. Does the teacher appear enthusiastic about the class?

2. Are lectures organized and presented clearly?

3. Are deadlines and responsibilities reasonable?

4. Are papers and exams returned to students in a reasonable amount of time?

5. Are comments on exams and papers instructive?

6. Is the instructor available outside of class?

7. Are office hours sufficient? Are they conveniently scheduled?

Evaluate the course content and reading.

1. Is the required reading useful for gaining an understanding of the course content?

2. Are the course themes clear?

3. What topics do you like the most and why?

4. What topics do you like the least and why?

Evaluate instructional methods.

1. How useful is each of the following methods used in the class: lecture, discussion, collaborative learning through groups, debates, simulations, oral presentations, videos. [List methods separately so students can comment on each.]
2. Do you have a reasonable amount of class time to ask questions?
3. Do the assignments help you to understand the subject?

Please suggest other teaching techniques that might be used in this class. Be as specific as possible.

Self-evaluation is an ongoing process in every teacher's career, from the graduate student teaching a first class to the instructor with thirty years' experience. Good teaching requires constant reflection on your preparation, your techniques, and your students' needs and interests.

EIGHT

TEACHING AS A GRADUATE STUDENT

Many, perhaps most, college and university teachers have their first classroom experience as graduate students. They may serve as readers or graders. They may teach discussion sections in a lecture course. They may teach undergraduate seminars of their own, advise research projects, even give lectures in their own sections of a survey course. Undergraduate education today, for better or worse, relies increasingly on graduate student teaching. And graduate student teachers, in addition to having to deal with all the normal issues that every teacher encounters, have to deal with particular issues related to being a student and a teacher at the same time.

Those issues are complicated by the fact that in many institutions graduate students enter the classroom without any advance training, without very much supervision, and with very limited feedback. For the most part, no one sees you teach other than your students, who—except in course evaluations—are not likely to comment to you on your performance. It is rare for faculty to visit graduate student classes (and very intimidating when they do). In many respects, you are entirely on your own. And yet in other respects, of course, you are not—because your teaching is part of a complicated relationship with your department and your own professors.

GUARDING YOUR TIME

Pursuing graduate education and teaching classes simultaneously is a constant juggling act. Good teaching, particularly at the beginning, can take as much time as or more time than your other graduate studies. Keeping the two careers in balance is not always easy. The main purpose of being in graduate school is to educate yourself, to build the foundation of a professional career. Teaching may be an integral part of that career, but it may not be the primary reason you wanted to get your doctorate. It is certainly not the only thing, or even the most important thing, in determining your professional future. So while you strive to be a good teacher, don't lose sight of the path to your degree.

That is not always an easy thing to do. Teaching will consume as much time and energy as you let it, particularly if you enjoy it. Budget your teaching time carefully so it does not intrude too heavily on your own work. The more organized your work schedule is, the less stressful your graduate experience, which is often stressful even without teaching, will be. Set aside particular days in which you prepare for the classes you teach and leave other days for your own coursework or dissertation research—and stick to the routine. Schedule office hours for the days when your classes meet so you will not have to spend more time on campus than is necessary. Obviously, you cannot plan for every contingency, and your schedule may go awry due to unexpected events. But you will enjoy teaching and research more, and make better progress on both, if you ration your time with care and conviction.

Remember also to relax. Getting away from both teaching and research is essential for your own mental well-being.

You will be happier and probably more efficient when you go back to work. Take at least a day and a night off every week. Socialize with friends or family. No matter how much time you think you ought to be spending preparing for the next class or locating one more citation for your research, if you do not allow unstructured time for yourself you will resent your work—and lose energy and enthusiasm for it. You can become a good teacher, student, and scholar without sacrificing your personal life.

RELATIONSHIPS WITH PROFESSORS

The most common way for graduate students to begin their teaching careers is to lead small discussion sections for a large lecture course. As a teaching assistant (TA), your role is set by the professor in whose course you are teaching, who may or may not give you the kind of guidance you expect and need. Some professors are active supervisors of their teaching assistants. They hold weekly meetings to coordinate section activities, and they get regular input from their TAs about all aspects of the course. Others give you the syllabus, expect you to come to lectures, and leave everything else to you. Still others hover between these two approaches. Whatever the situation you encounter, you will, of course, want to get as much as you can out of your teaching experience, do as well as you can for your students, and maintain a professional relationship with the professor in charge—all at the same time.

The best way to do that is to understand your position. Remember that as a teaching assistant, you are in charge of your section but not of the course as a whole. No matter how much you dislike a book on the syllabus or the topics of a required paper or the contents of a lecture by the professor, it is still your responsibility to teach them carefully and with commitment and to try to explain to the students why the assignment or the material is important to the course. Many professors will ask their TAs for advice, and at that point, it is appropriate to offer your observations about some of the drawbacks and strengths of various aspects of the course. But on the whole, you must live with the professor's decisions about the structure of the course and try to make the best of them.

As you begin new teaching assignments, be sure to clarify your duties and responsibilities with your professors. What are the professors' goals for the discussion sections? What do they expect of their TAs? Are you expected to attend every lecture, even if you have listened to the lectures in the same course before? Are you expected to grade all the papers? Give reading quizzes regularly? Hold extra review sessions before exams? While most professors explain the various parts of the job to TAs before the beginning of the term, some just assume you will know what you are supposed to do. To avoid problems later, ask about your specific duties before the course begins. No doubt you will find yourself doing more than you anticipated, but at least you will have a sense of what to expect.

If possible, meet regularly with the professor to discuss the progress of the course. If you are working with a professor who meets with TAs every week or so, use these meetings to clarify questions of subject matter, exchange teaching ideas, and obtain guidance on any classroom problems you might be having. If the professor does not hold such meetings, you might suggest that he or she do so; or, with the professor's approval, you might try to organize the TAs into their own group that will meet together to discuss teaching every week. Even if there is no weekly meeting, find some other occasion—office hours, before or after class—to ask the professor for help and guidance if you need it.

Because TAs seldom have the luxury of choosing for whom they will work, there are inevitable personality clashes or differences of opinion at times over matters such as teaching methodology or grading standards. Indeed, you may find yourself assisting a professor with whom you have had an unpleasant experience as a graduate student. Often you will have no choice but to act like a professional and do your best. If difficulties arise which inhibit your teaching ability, however, speak directly to the professor. As awkward as such a conversation might be, it is almost always better to clear the air rather than let your frustration and anger build—and possibly infect your relations with your students. If problems persist, talk to your adviser, the department's faculty member in charge of TAs (if there is one), or the department chair. If problems are particularly serious, you might wish to seek outside help, perhaps from graduate student organizations or the campus teaching center. There is usually a very large imbalance of power in your relationship with the professor in charge of your course, particularly if the professor is important to your future in other ways. It is important, therefore, to manage your relationship with the instructor carefully and to ask for help when you need it.

RELATIONSHIPS WITH STUDENTS

Graduate student instructors also face special issues in their relationships with their students because the instructors are in an unusual position in the professional hierarchy of the university. If you are a graduate teaching assistant, you are not just a teacher to your students; you are also their intermediary with the professor. If you teach your own class, you take on the role of a professor, but without the status of a regular faculty member. Your students may or may not be aware of your position within the university, but you, of course, will be. And you will be rightly concerned about conducting yourself in a way that will meet with the approval of your faculty supervisors while also meeting the needs of your students. Whatever position you occupy, you need to conduct yourself in a professional manner with your colleagues and, most importantly, your students. Striving for a friendly yet professional relationship with them is a crucial part of teaching.

Whether you are a teaching assistant or an instructor in charge of your own course, your position gives you a certain amount of power and authority in and out of the classroom. No matter how friendly you are with your students, you should not forget that your relationship is not one of absolute or even relative equality. You should be friendly toward your students, but you should also maintain a professional distance from them. You may not be very much older than they are, but it is your job to represent to them, and encourage them to develop, a strong commitment to intellectual life and a sincere interest in their education.

Insist on mutual respect in the classroom—both in your relationship with your students, and in their relationships with one another. Treat your students with fairness and respect. Do not intimidate them with intellectual or disciplinary authority. Intervene quickly when students are behaving inappropriately toward each other. Welcome them during office hours and listen to their academic concerns. Treat them all equally, without favoritism.

Create an atmosphere of tolerance in your classroom. In social science and humanities disciplines, it is common to discuss sensitive topics, among them issues of race, ethnicity, gender, sexuality, politics, and religion. Encourage respect for alternative viewpoints through listening, questioning, and reasoned argument. No doubt most of your students will have strong opinions, but remind them that convincing opinions—and good scholarship—stem from sound logic and reliable evidence. Try to use such discussions to further students' understanding of the process of scholarly inquiry.

Clarify your expectations and rules early in the term. Students want to know what you expect of them in the course and in the classroom. The course requirements are listed on the syllabus. What you need to establish during the first few meetings are the tone and atmosphere of your own class. How much structure will you build into discussions? Does a student need to raise her hand if she wants to make a comment? Will you tolerate late arrivals and early departures? Will you allow students to eat in class?

If you are a teaching assistant in a course taught by a professor, you need to decide how you wish to position yourself in relation to what the professor has to say in lectures or through the assigned readings. You should not feel obliged to agree with everything the professor says, and if your students ask you your views on an issue, you should answer honestly. On the other hand, you should not position yourself as the professor's antagonist, and you should express any disagreements in a tempered way—making clear that you have respect for the point of view with which you disagree.

RESOLVING DISPUTES WITH STUDENTS

You will likely find yourself in disputes at times with individual students over such issues as grades, behavior, academic honesty, or personality. Because you are probably going to see your students every week through an entire term, it is usually best to confront such problems rather than hope they will go away by themselves.

If you have a personal disagreement with a student, talk to him or her about it before it gets worse. Try to work out an agreeable solution that clears the air and will not inhibit the student's learning or your teaching. Remember that it is unlikely that you will please all students all the time. Do not interpret this as a personal failure. You do want your students to enjoy coming to class and even to like you. But you cannot compromise your responsibilities to the course, to your students, and to yourself to achieve that goal.

If a student is rude or obstreperous to other students, speak to him or her the first time it happens. It is probably best to acknowledge such behavior in class simply by cutting the student off, hopefully in a way that will not embarrass the offender. If the behavior recurs, speak to the student after class and explain calmly but firmly why you find the behavior unacceptable. In any case, do not let it go unnoticed because it may become worse.

A more common problem is complaints about grades. Students will be aware that you, not the professor, are grading their work. They may also be aware of the grade scale that other teaching assistants in the same course are using. It is tempting to look scornfully at students who protest their grades. But you should recall that students are under tremendous pressure to maintain high grade point averages to position themselves well for jobs or graduate schools. And you should also keep in mind that sometimes their complaints are justified. You should, therefore, take grade grievances seriously. You can preempt some problems by clearly explaining your criteria for evaluating specific papers, assignments, and exams in advance. But no amount of forethought will eliminate all complaints. So give the student a fair hearing. Then explain clearly and with specific examples why he or she earned that particular grade. Whether or not you reread the paper or exam and revise the grade depends on the policy you or the professor has set for the course as a whole. In any event, remain consistent when further grievances arise. If the student remains unsatisfied, suggest that he or she take the paper or exam to the professor in charge of the course (providing that the professor is willing to consider such complaints). You should not feel that a student who appeals your grade is undermining your authority. The professor is the ultimate authority, and it is reasonable for students to expect a hearing from him or her.

PLAGIARISM AND CHEATING

Plagiarism is the most difficult and painful grievance to arise between teachers and students, and it becomes a particularly difficult issue if you are a graduate student without the full authority of your institution behind you. You should, of course, try to prevent the problem by discussing it early in the course and, if you have reason to think it may be a problem, giving a clear explanation of what constitutes plagiarism. But if you do encounter plagiarism, you need to think not just about the student, but about yourself. Do you have the authority to deal with the issue on your own? If you are a TA in a course taught by a professor, you should bring any such problems to the professor's attention. If the professor asks you to handle it, then you should do so in the same way an instructor of any rank would proceed (see chapter 5). But be sure you have the authority to act before you become embroiled in what will likely be a very unpleasant and difficult dispute. A graduate student is not usually in a very strong position to deal with so explosive a problem. If someone else—a professor, a committee, an administrator—can handle the problem for you, it is usually best to pass the problem on.

The same principles apply to suspected cheating on examinations. Consult with your professor or your department about how they wish such issues to be handled. Pass on responsibility for handling it if you can. But do not permit cheating to continue without a response, and if necessary take steps on your own to deal with it.

If the decision about how to deal with plagiarism or cheating is yours alone, you have a number of options, ranging from simply failing the student on the work in question or in the course as a whole (and explaining why) to giving the student a chance to do the work over. If you or your professor has set a clear policy at the beginning of the term (for example, any work that involves plagiarism will be failed), stick to it. If you have not, evaluate the seriousness of the problem and what you can observe about the motives of the student before deciding how to respond. Before you do anything, be sure to listen to the student's point of view. And be prepared for an emotional response that may run the gamut from indignation and denial to tears and remorse.

ETHICAL DILEMMAS

Sometimes your dual role as teacher and student may leave you with a sense of divided loyalties, uncertain about where your professional responsibilities lie. The position of teaching assistant can become even stickier since the students think of you as the buffer between them and the professor. Students may see you as a personal confidant rather than as a teacher. You may be tempted to consider some members of your classes to be friends as much as students. It is important, therefore, to establish ground rules for your relationships with students to avoid the possibility of awkwardness, embarrassment, or worse.

Maintain a professional distance from your students. Listen to their academic concerns but do not try to become their psychoanalyst or their parent. You are unlikely to be qualified to help students with serious psychological or personal problems—and you may cause more harm than good if you try. If students have such problems, refer them to the appropriate professional resources on or off campus.

Never become romantically involved with one of your students. The line between friendly behavior and what might be considered impropriety or sexual harassment is a fine one, but you should never cross or even approach it. Schools and universities usually have very strict rules about what constitutes an improper relationship or sexual harassment, and such rules may include behavior that falls far short of the legal definition. Follow those rules rigorously, even if they seem excessively strict. After the course has concluded, you should still avoid becoming personally involved with any of your former students for a significant period of time to avoid creating a perception of impropriety within your institution that could be harmful to you both.

If your institution has no guidelines regarding improper relationships, use common sense. Avoid meeting students alone in your home or theirs. Avoid unusual physical contact. Make sure not to make comments or use language that might be interpreted as flirtatious or provocative. It is usually unwise, for example, to comment on a student's clothes or hairstyle. Sensitivities are high in today's world on matters of sexuality and intimacy, and whether or not you believe such sensitivities are justified you must be aware of them and be careful not to offend them. You can pay a heavy price for failing to do so.

Always conduct yourself in a professional manner with fellow graduate students and faculty as well. Making a personal criticism of a professor or another TA to your students, your fellow TAs, or other faculty is unprofessional. Always keep the confidences of faculty, fellow TAs, and most of all your students.

Keep grades confidential. Never discuss student grades or other personal information with students, TAs, or faculty other than the professor in charge of your course.

Respond seriously to student complaints about professors. Obviously, this calls for tact and timing, and for an evaluation of the character of the professor involved and your relationship with him or her. But if students have complaints that you think are justified, it is usually a good idea to relay them to the professor—making clear that the suggestions are coming from students, and that your goal is to be helpful. If you meet regularly with the professor along with other TAs, such a meeting may be a good time to bring up problems that students have mentioned. That way, you can create a discussion of it among colleagues rather than a possible confrontation with a professor. You alone, however, must decide whether the consequences to you of bringing a complaint to a professor's attention are likely to outweigh the value of airing grievances. Here, as in many other cases, you must balance your own stake in your relationship with a professor against what you think your responsibilities to your students are.

Avoid departmental politics. Every department, no matter how cooperative and friendly, has its own internal controversies that divide the faculty and create problems that sometimes spill over to graduate students. Some, like the issue of graduate student unionization that has emerged recently in some universities, will affect you directly. Others, such as hiring decisions, may have only a peripheral impact. In either case, remember that your main purpose in graduate school is to get an education. If you do get involved in a controversial issue, try to do it in a quiet and professional way and try to avoid being emotional or confrontational. You are in a vulnerable position as a graduate student, and direct confrontations with faculty can be very damaging to your future. Avoid such confrontations unless you believe your personal or academic integrity is at stake.

TEACHING AND CAREER PLACEMENT

Once you are near the end of your graduate education and the job market looms on the horizon, the place of teaching in your professional training takes on a new dimension. In the tight market most graduate students face today, potential employers have become more demanding of their candidates. Except at the most elite research universities (and not invariably there either), scholarly credentials—your dissertation and other written work—are usually not enough. In liberal arts colleges, state universities, and community colleges, where most of the jobs are, teaching is often more important than research. Prospective employers may thus be more interested in your potential as a teacher than in your scholarly accomplishments. It is not uncommon for both universities and colleges to ask a candidate to teach a class as part of the campus interview. You should, therefore, consider ways in which your teaching experience can give you an edge in the job market.

The most obvious way to prepare for the job market is in preparing your dossier. Be sure that at least one of your references addresses your teaching ability. Such a reference should come from someone with whom, or for whom, you have taught, and ideally from someone who has evaluated your teaching and with whom you have discussed techniques and course planning. If you have been a TA, ask your supervising professor.

Think seriously about how you will discuss teaching in a job interview. Interviewers will almost certainly address teaching, even in a preliminary interview held at a professional meeting. Be prepared to outline some of the following to potential employers:

- kinds of classes you have already taught, those you feel capable of teaching, and those you would particularly like to teach
- particular teaching techniques you have developed that might suggest your talents in the classroom, kinds of assignments you have created for students
- plans for how you would teach graduate courses (if you are interviewing for a position in a university with a graduate program)

- books you would use in particular courses
- ways you might incorporate your own research into your teaching

Many graduate students keep a formal record of their teaching career to use in the job search. You should consider beginning a portfolio as soon as you start teaching and adding to it as you progress through various courses. A portfolio should include syllabi from courses in which you have taught (and any hypothetical syllabi you may have prepared for courses you would like to teach). It should also include examples of different types of assignments you have given students, particularly successful ones, along with an explanation of the rationale behind the assignments. Your portfolio might also include the results of student evaluations of your teaching, if they have been statistically compiled in a form available to you, or even a sample of the actual evaluation forms, which your department may keep on file. Include as well a short statement describing your teaching techniques, philosophy, or goals. If you have one, you might make available a short videotape of yourself in the classroom.

If you do decide to create a teaching portfolio, it will, of course, reflect your own experiences and interests and may not include precisely the items suggested here. Whatever kind of portfolio you create, try to make it flexible. Different potential employers will have different teaching needs, and you should tailor your credentials to the particular characteristics of the job. There is nothing dishonest about this as long as the credentials are accurately presented. An elite research university might expect evidence of different kinds of teaching talents than would be required at a small college, for example, and it is perfectly appropriate to present yourself in the most suitable light for each circumstance.

Teaching portfolios are not an ordinary part of an application, and you should not send one to potential employers unsolicited—just as you normally would not send chapters of your dissertation until requested to do so. Mention it in your application letter as one of the things you will send on request. If you are invited to a campus interview later on, take it with you (if you have not previously submitted it) and look for an appropriate moment at which to introduce it.

Teaching as a graduate student is often extraordinarily rewarding—and often a great deal of fun. It can also be difficult and awkward. Whatever the experience, you should try to act professionally, serve your students well, and draw from your teaching whatever lessons (and professional benefits) you can for the future.

NINE

TEACHING
INCLUSIVELY
IN A MULTI-
CULTURAL AGE

Teaching in today's world is, and will continue to be, very different from teaching a generation or more ago. In the past, teachers had unquestioned authority in most classrooms; today that authority is likely to be contested in many ways. In the past, most schools and universities had relatively homogeneous student bodies; today, most classrooms are coeducational, multiethnic, and multiracial. In the past, most teaching occurred in the context of a few, traditional disciplines; today, teachers must adapt to a host of new areas of academic interest.

The reasons for these changes are not difficult to see: the end of legalized segregation; the rise of feminism; the increasing self-consciousness of racial, ethnic, and sexual minorities; a new legal and cultural climate that gives power and legitimacy to the demands of minorities; new waves of immigration, which have made our culture even more diverse than it has been in the recent past; heightened conceptions of individual rights and liberties.

The impact of these developments on America's classrooms has been considerable. There are new academic programs in fields as varied as African-American studies; women's and gender studies; Latino, Native American, Asian-

American studies; gay and lesbian studies. And there are many other new programs examining the influence of race, gender, ethnicity, region, and religion on the lives of Americans. Today's diverse student bodies and curricula demand new techniques and new sensitivities from educators who wish to engage all of their students successfully. "Multiculturalism" has become a controversial concept in American politics and culture. But for most teachers in most institutions, it is a simple reality that cannot be ignored.

MEETING YOUR STUDENTS

Issues of diversity may arise as early as the first meeting of a class. Students may, for various reasons, be wary when they first encounter you, and you can do a great deal at the beginning to make them feel at ease.

An important first step is to make an effort to pronounce students' names correctly. Calling roll for the first time without mispronouncing unfamiliar names is a challenge. But getting it right is important since it demonstrates the teacher's respect for, and appreciation of, the diverse backgrounds of their students. Never make a joke about a name that is difficult to pronounce. If you are having trouble with names, ask the students very simply and straightforwardly how to pronounce them correctly.

Do what it takes to attach names to faces if your class is not too large. This is something you should do with all your students, needless to say, but it can be especially important to minority students. One teacher has noted an experience that illustrates the importance of this seemingly obvious issue. She recalls that there were two African-American students who always sat together in the back of her class. She was very careful to learn their names and to address them directly when she called on them. One day one of the young men spoke to her after class. He thanked her for making the effort to learn his name. He explained that in a previous class where the instructor had always confused him with his friend, he had felt alienated. But now he felt like a part of the class simply because she had made the effort to learn who he was.

Encourage your students to introduce themselves and, if they wish to do so, say something about their backgrounds and what perspectives they bring to the material you are examining. This has the advantage of establishing an atmosphere of openness from the beginning and of helping students to feel more comfortable with the diversity within the group.

CHALLENGES OF DIVERSITY

In a multicultural society, dialogues about race, ethnicity, gender, and sexuality have many dangers. The subjects are charged; sensitivities are high. The potential for misunderstanding is large. But dancing around such dialogues has dangers as well. Effective teaching requires confronting diversity without allowing it to overwhelm your shared intellectual project.

Exploit the opportunities that diversity presents for vigorous and lively exchanges. In many instances, students of different backgrounds are curious about each other. When appropriate, use this curiosity to enable students to learn from each other. No students should be expected or required to become spokespeople for particular groups or to say anything at all about their backgrounds. But students who wish to speak about their own perspectives should be encouraged to explain how their background has shaped the way they view material.

Confront difficult student assumptions—and the problems they may raise—quickly, directly, and sensitively. Consider the experience of a young white instructor at a historically black private liberal arts college. When he started teaching, he was asked to teach an African-American history survey. He felt comfortable with the idea of teaching the course at first—until he met the students, almost all of them black, who greeted his arrival with an uneasy silence accompanied by a variety of facial expressions that ranged from the quizzical to the hostile. Before he could even open his mouth, one of the black students demanded to know, "What gives you the right to teach us our history?" The teacher realized that if he did not reach those students immediately, he probably would never reach them. He paused, took a deep breath, and then—aware that the issue was on everyone's mind— he asked the same question back to the class: "Do *you* think white people can teach African-American history?" That started a discussion that helped to clear the air. As the students voiced their opinions, the tension began to ebb from the room. This set the tone for a more comfortable atmosphere during the whole term, one based on mutual respect and understanding.

Confront your own prejudices or biases, which may be subtle or even invisible to you. An African-American teacher from the Midwest, for example, remembers her first experience in a classroom in the South looking out at a sea of southern white faces. Remembering her image of the South from a childhood spent watching racial confrontations in Birmingham and elsewhere, she automatically made assumptions about their attitudes toward, and their experiences with, race. But once she began to listen to her students—almost all of whom had been born after the events she recalled and had no memory of them—she learned that her assumptions revealed much more about her thinking than about theirs. You should not discuss your biases in a public forum. But you should reflect on them privately at some point—and the sooner the better, for your students and yourself.

Be open to queries and challenges from your students that may reveal to you aspects of your teaching of which you are unaware. Consider the experience a decade ago of a white male professor at an eastern university who had recently given a lecture on liberation movements in the 1960s. A few days later, a student came to his office and very politely asked why, in listing such movements, he had not mentioned gay liberation. The professor's first instinct was to be defensive, but he quickly realized that it was a perfectly legitimate question and that the only appropriate response was to say that he certainly should have mentioned it, was sorry he had not, and appreciated the reminder. Similar queries come often from students in today's changing academic world, and you should always remain open to comments that may alert you to aspects of your subject that you may never have considered, that perhaps were not on anyone's mind when you began teaching a course, but that now deserve a place in your curriculum. Even a very brief reference to an area of study that is important to some group of your students can help make them feel included and can give their own concerns a sense of legitimacy.

Most of all, remember that the race, ethnicity, gender, or sexual orientation of your students is first and foremost their own business. If they choose to bring their backgrounds to bear on a discussion or a project in your class, make them feel comfortable doing so. If they choose to draw no attention to their backgrounds, you should not do so either. A female student should not be assumed to be an expert on feminism unless she herself chooses to make the claim that she is. An African-American student should not be expected to have anything more to say about an issue involving race than a white student would be. You should try to create an environment in which diversity does not make your students feel uncomfortable. That means both giving students a chance to talk about their backgrounds openly and freely if they wish, and also making it possible for them to make no reference to their backgrounds at all if they do not wish to do so.

OPPORTUNITIES OF
DIVERSITY

Teaching inclusively is the same as teaching well. You should not think of diversity as a problem, or even a challenge— although under some circumstances it can be both. You should think of it above all as a fact and an opportunity. And you should take steps not just to avoid pitfalls but to use diversity creatively.

Consider the kind of knowledge students from various backgrounds bring to your class. Their knowledge may come from formal education or from informal experience, or more likely from both, and you should try to find ways to allow both kinds of knowledge to be expressed. But beware of assuming that students possess more information than they actually do. Minority students are no more likely than any other students to have preexisting knowledge of the history or politics or sociology or literature of their communities. You should, therefore, reevaluate regularly what shared bodies of knowledge and what collective memories are available in your classroom at a given moment.

At the same time, do not underestimate the way in which contemporary experience and popular culture can become the basis for shared conversation. Look for opportunities to involve people or organizations from your community in classroom discussions when they can bring their own experiences to bear on the efforts of students to understand difficult issues.

Remember, too, that whatever you are teaching, your students are taking other courses as well. In a racially or ethnically diverse class, you should pay attention to what else your students are studying and think about making some connections between what you are teaching and what they are learning elsewhere. If you are teaching a course on American fiction and you know that some of your students are studying African-American literature, think about sug-

gesting some of the ways the two fields of study are linked
to one another—not just by assigning works by African-
American writers, which you would probably naturally do
in any case, but by suggesting ways in which black and white
literature have influenced one another.

"POLITICAL CORRECTNESS"

The idea, and at times the reality, of "political correctness"
has become a major source of controversy and debate in academia, and in American culture generally. Political correctness is a derisive term coined some years ago to describe the
way in which people tailor their speech and even their
thought to what they assume is expected of them by other
groups. It is generally identified with academia, and with lib-
erals and the left, and it is widely assumed by people outside
the academy to be a major problem in the educational
world—particularly for people with relatively conservative
beliefs.

It is certainly true that there are many examples of political correctness that should dismay, even horrify, any reasonable person. Academia requires an unusual degree of openness and toleration, and no one should be required to adopt
views simply because they are fashionable—or to avoid ex-
pressing views just because they might make some students
feel uncomfortable. Feeling uncomfortable is often part of
learning new and difficult things.

But just as defenders of political correctness sometimes
make unreasonable demands of their teachers, critics of political correctness are often equally unreasonable in making
their own claims. Much of what is dismissed as political correctness is, in fact, simple sensitivity to the way in which the
world has changed. Few instructors today would refer to
African-Americans as "colored" or even "Negro," even though
such terms were considered widely acceptable a generation

or more ago. Almost everyone uses instead the terms that have become conventional today—black, African-American, "people of color." Most teachers and writers no longer use the word "men" to describe groups that in fact include women, or use masculine pronouns to refer generically to people—even though both such practices were common in the past. Using gender-neutral language sometimes creates some grammatical awkwardness and requires a modest amount of creativity, but it is now an almost universally accepted practice both inside and outside the academy. Language changes with the times; clinging to old practices in the face of broad social transformations that have made those practices obsolete is not a defense of standards, but stubbornness.

It would be nice to think that there was never a time when teachers used demeaning terms for minority groups or told ethnic or racist or sexist jokes in class, but of course some teachers often did such things in the past. Many of the most painful incidents of teachers finding themselves under attack for insensitivity involve casual, sometimes unthinking, use of such language or stories in classes today. It should go without saying that you should never use an ethnic or sexist slur, and that you should make distinctions between language that you might be exposed to routinely in your nonacademic life and language that is appropriate in the classroom. It should be equally clear that you should never tell a story or a joke that makes fun of any racial or ethnic group, or that makes use of sexist stereotypes.

More difficult is deciding how to handle such language, stories, or jokes when they appear in material with which you are teaching. One famous example is the film *The Birth of a Nation*, the great D. W. Griffith epic that remains a landmark in the history of American filmmaking. It is also an offensively reactionary and racist movie that glorifies the Ku Klux Klan and presents demeaning stereotypes of black southerners in the years following the Civil War. For many years, the

film was considered so controversial that most teachers re-
fused to screen it; those who did were likely to encounter
very strong and angry protests from many of their students.
Gradually, however, teachers who wished to use the film
learned how to present it in a way that made clear its importance as a film without overlooking its simultaneous importance as a historical document that reveals painful prejudices and stereotypes that were once common among white
Americans.

Students should not be shielded from material that reveals to them unpleasant and offensive aspects of human existence if it is also material that is important in some other
way, or if it can be helpful to them in understanding an issue
of significance. But that material must be presented to them
in context, in a way that makes it possible for them to discuss
it without having to endorse it. That means making sure to
warn students in advance that the material may seem offensive; explaining to them what its academic significance is;
and encouraging them to speak openly about the biases and
prejudices they encounter in it.

It is also important to help students understand the difference between material that is itself biased and material
that attempts to examine and understand prejudice. A striking example of the failure to make such a distinction is the
effort in recent years by a few communities to remove Mark
Twain's novel *The Adventures of Huckleberry Finn* from school
libraries and student reading lists. *Huckleberry Finn* is one of
the greatest and most important of all American novels. It
contains a brilliant, if easily misunderstood, discussion of racial prejudice, which an unwary reader might consider an
endorsement of racism. In fact, Twain, like many other writers, addressed prejudice and hatred directly in his novel, in
an effort to help society confront and overcome them. Today's students should not shy away from such efforts just
because they may create discomfort. Such work is designed
to make readers uncomfortable. You should prepare your

students carefully when you are presenting material of this kind to them and talk openly about whatever is controversial in the material, but never shy away from it.

Political correctness is not a figment of the right's imagination. But neither is it the powerful and corrosive force in academia that many critics claim it is. A reasonable openness to new ideas, new forms of scholarship, and changes in language—and a reasonable attention to the likely sensitivities of your students—should be a basic part of your teaching whatever the surrounding political climate. Taking care to be open and tolerant is not being "politically correct." It is being a good teacher.

TEN

USING
ELECTRONIC
RESOURCES FOR
TEACHING

Computers and related electronic resources have come to play a central role in education. Whatever your feelings about what some have called the digital revolution, you must accept that many, perhaps most, of your students are fully immersed in it. At the very simplest level, you will rarely receive a paper or other assignment from a student that has not been written with the help of a computer. Most of your students will have considerable experience with the Internet and will, whether you like it or not, make use of it for much of their academic work. Many of them will be accustomed to using e-mail as a normal form of communication. But it is not just students who find electronic resources valuable. Teachers can benefit from these resources as well, by employing a series of useful tools.

We stress the word "useful" because electronic resources complement, but seldom replace, more conventional teaching techniques. Electronic tools can make classes more efficient; lectures more compelling, informative, and varied; reading assignments more extensive, interesting, and accessible; discussions more free ranging and challenging; and students' papers more original and well researched. Only you, how-

ever, can judge if these techniques advance your own teaching goals.

FIVE PROMISING USES OF
NEW TECHNOLOGY

Of the many electronic teaching techniques that instructors
have found useful, we have chosen five that we believe seem
particularly likely to help significant numbers of teachers. All
of these techniques demand an investment of time if they
are to succeed, and your willingness to use them should be
balanced carefully against other, perhaps more important,
teaching priorities. But for each technique, there are both simple and complex ways of proceeding, and we will try to make
clear the respective advantages and disadvantages.

The five ways in which we suggest teachers consider using electronic resources involve tasks that you will usually
have to perform in any case. New technologies can help you
perform them better and more easily:

- *Administration:* The routine administration of
  courses (advertising a class, providing copies of
  the syllabus, assigning discussion sections, and
  getting out course news) can be more efficiently
  handled with a course home page, electronic discussion groups, and e-mail lists. These tools can
  also dramatically improve the continuity and the
  community aspects of courses, helping students
  to engage with and learn from each other and
  even from people outside the course.
- *Readings/sources:* The Web and CD-ROMs provide a wider variety of secondary and primary
  sources (including visual and audio sources)
  than has previously been available. With your
  guidance, your students can now gain access to

materials that were once accessible only to experts because they were too cumbersome to reproduce for classroom use or too expensive for students to purchase. By taking their own paths through these sources, students can bring their own evidence and arguments into lectures and discussion sections, as well as write on a wider range of research topics.

- *Papers/presentations:* Rather than receiving assignments and taking exams from the teacher alone, students can perform more independent exercises in publishing, exhibit building, or assembling and presenting teaching units and other materials for their peers. A web archive of several terms' work can make the course itself an ongoing and collaborative intellectual construction.

- *Lectures:* A computer with presentation software can provide a single tool for augmenting lectures with outlines, slides, statistical charts and tables, images, music, and even video clips. In addition to printing them as handouts, you can save in-class presentations in a web-compatible format for later review and discussion.

- *Discussion:* Electronic discussion tools such as e-mail, conferencing software, and on-line chat services can seed discussion questions before the class meets, draw out your shy students, and follow up on discussions or questions on the reading between classes. For courses without face-to-face discussion sections, these tools can bring the course to life over great distances and help overcome scheduling difficulties.

In the sections below, we discuss each of these techniques and how you might consider using them.

THE NECESSARY TOOLS

What you need will depend, of course, on what you want to do. Most teachers have computers, and most have at least some access to e-mail and the Internet. In many schools and universities, most students do, too. Many teaching opportunities are likely to be available to you, therefore, using equipment you and your students already have. Other techniques require more advanced technologies that you may or may not wish to purchase on your own, and that your institution may or may not make available to you. It should be obvious, therefore, that you should make no plans for using electronic tools before making sure that both you and your students will have access to the necessary technology.

But owning, or having access to, technology is usually only a first step. Even more important is learning how to use it. This is one of the biggest challenges facing anyone who wishes to use electronic tools, because the knowledge is not always easy to acquire. Many people, of course, are highly skilled in computer technology and know how to teach themselves to do almost anything. But many other people have limited computer skills, are easily intimidated by new and unfamiliar tasks, and tend to avoid doing anything that requires them to learn something very different from the things to which they are accustomed. If you fall in the latter group but wish to expand your ability to use electronic tools, you need to find help. Some institutions offer extensive assistance through their computer centers or their information technology services. Some departments have staff members or graduate student assistants who are hired to handle computer-related problems. There are also many excellent reference works to help you learn about various electronic tools. Just as you must be sure that you have the necessary technology at your disposal before you decide to use electronic tools in your teaching, so you must also make sure that you have access to the necessary help in learning to use it.

Keep in mind, finally, that the technology associated with computers and the Internet changes with breathtaking speed. Although certain skills will remain useful to you over long periods of time, there will be many things that will have to be relearned time and time again. The rapidity of change in this field can be bewildering and intimidating. But it is also the source of some valuable innovations that can be of great use to you.

Before introducing new teaching techniques, therefore, it is wise to make a quick inventory of your own and your school's electronic teaching resources. You will not want to discover halfway through a project that there are major obstacles such as insufficient equipment, inadequate support, or negative professional incentives. Answering a few simple questions can help you determine how practical and promising potential innovations in electronic teaching are likely to be. While some answers may lie as close as your departmental colleagues, others might require conferring with departmental administrators, librarians, or computer support organizations.

- Does your school have a web page? What courses have material on-line? Which departments and faculty have web pages? Where are they stored? (One source for help in understanding how your institution's web site works is the person who is in charge of constructing it, usually known as the *webmaster*. If your school has a web site, look at the bottom of the home page or on the credits page of the site to find the e-mail address of your webmaster.)

- What kinds of computers and Internet access do students have? Do most students own their own computers? If not, are there long waits for access? Twenty-four-hour computer labs? Provisions for off-campus students? What software is on these computers? And what Internet browser (and version) do students typically use?

- Has your school purchased or is it planning to purchase a standard software package to manage the creation of course web pages? These tools offer simple fill-in-the-blank on-line forms to allow you to place standard course material on the Internet, after which the program creates the course home page for you. If not, is there a school style sheet or recommended format for course pages? Does your school recommend or support any particular software for web pages? For presentations, word processing, spreadsheets, and databases?

- What staff is available to assist instructors with educational technology? Are there any work-study students or teaching assistants trained for new media support? What handouts or on-line guides have been prepared for electronic teaching?

- Are there particular classrooms designed for multimedia presentations? Do any classrooms have Internet access? Are classes that are making use of this technology given extra technical or financial support?

- Are there special funds or professional recognition for innovative uses of technology in teaching? Are any of your colleagues working on grants that support electronic teaching? What is the attitude of your department and of school officials to this activity?

- Does your institution have a plan for on-line course materials? Does the school have distance learning plans (methods by which students with on-line access can take courses remotely)? How is your department's teaching and funding going to be affected by these plans?

- What can you use on the Internet? The new media is so new that no clear guidelines have been established for determining fair use and copyright policies for on-line teaching materials. In general, however, the same copyright rules that govern photocopied packets and other more familiar teaching tools are likely to apply to on-line material. You should, however, identify the office or officer at your institution responsible for monitoring such policies.
- Will your on-line materials belong to you? Investigate your institution's policies (or ask for one to be made) on whether you or the school owns your on-line materials. This is especially important if you are investing considerable creative time and energy, making heavy use of university equipment and staff, or may wish to take the material with you to another institution.

THE COURSE HOME PAGE

A course home page can serve several functions. Even before the course begins, it can advertise your course to prospective students. Before and during the term it can reduce demand for paper copies of course materials. More importantly, it can present a broader range of material than paper handouts would by including multimedia material and on-line sources. As its name implies, a home page can act as a twenty-four-hour communications center for news, assignments, and discussions. Indeed, it can play host to the four other electronic techniques discussed below.

Before you create a home page for your course, you

should first carefully define its scope and content. It is best to start simply and enhance your site in stages to benefit from experience and feedback. The simplest sites consist of a single page reproducing the traditional paper syllabus. The next, more useful level includes separate pages or sections for paper assignments, section lists, and hyperlinks to readings and sources. The most advanced sites, such as those for distance learning courses, can include all the materials needed for the course: lectures, readings, audio and video recordings, exams, and evaluations.

As with most projects, a good outline and definition of your web site can save many hours of revisions and false starts. Ask a few basic questions before you start:

- What are the goals of your site? Is it going to perform administrative chores? Advertise the course? Introduce unique materials? Publish and archive student work? Answers to these questions should shape the design and scope of your site.
- What are the features you like and dislike about existing course sites at your school and on the Internet? What institutional support, standards, and tools might guide your efforts?
- What traditional materials will go on the site? Syllabus, assignments, handouts, bibliographies, slides, maps?
- What multimedia or otherwise cumbersome material might be easily included on a web page? Sound recordings, images, video, statistical data?
- Which of your readings are available or could be made available on-line? Are there reputable Internet sources on a particular topic? Can you scan material into your site without violating copyright laws?
- Will the home page host student publications, lecture materials, or on-line discussions?

- Which of these items is essential to meeting your goals? Which could be saved for a second, third, or fourth stage? Which have little educational value and should be dropped?
- What are logical divisions for all this material? Home pages should usually limit their initial menus to seven or fewer choices.

When you set out actually to create a course home page, you will have a number of methods from which to choose. You may have access to someone expert at transferring material from word processing files to a web-compatible format; in this case, prepare your material using a word processor, making sure to use simple formatting that will translate easily to the Web. (Italics and bold are best; underlining can create problems.) Then give it to whoever is transferring the material to your web site. If you are constructing the web page yourself, look for assistance—in computer manuals or from a knowledgeable colleague or student—in using the various editing tools available. These may include schoolwide fill-in-the-blanks courseware; a word processor capable of opening and saving files in HTML (Hypertext Markup Language), the computer language in which web pages are written; a simple text editor for working directly in HTML; or specialized HTML editors such as Microsoft FrontPage or Netscape Composer, which provide a word processor–like interface for composing pages.

The most successful course web sites use the unique capabilities of the medium to provide material not available to students in other forms. This could include hyperlinks (words or phrases, usually in a different color type, which will take students to other web sites with a simple click of the mouse button) to on-line readings, lecture outlines, or even sample exam questions that are not otherwise distributed to the class.

Whether you have constructed your web site yourself or had someone else do it for you, you should proofread your pages very carefully, test to make sure all the links work, and keep a careful eye on the overall size of your pages and individual images. Because web sites often look different on various computers, you should also try to view your pages in as many different browsers as possible, especially in the Macintosh and Windows computer labs that the students might be using. If you have students who commute to campus, you should try to get access to your course materials from off campus using a modem (which connects computers to the Internet using a telephone line) to ensure that your pages and graphics can be displayed efficiently on computers not directly connected to your institution's network.

Once you have constructed a web site, make an effort to publicize it. Be sure that it is listed in all the proper places on your school's web site—that there are clear links to it from, for example, your department's home page. Put the site's Internet address (known as a *URL*) on your paper course materials. Describe the site to your students on the first few days of class, write the URL on the board, and indicate whether and where they can get help finding and using the Web.

ELECTRONIC SOURCES

For the moment, at least, textbooks and monographs have little to fear from on-line competition. Few students or faculty will submit to reading long passages of text on a computer screen. But many classrooms can benefit from electronic resources in at least two areas: supplementary readings and primary sources. Even the best published readers or photocopied packets tend to dampen the thrill of discovery because they have been preselected and packaged for a particular purpose (seldom your own). Electronic sources, whether on CD-ROM or the Web, can significantly open up the range of materials accessible to your students.

There are a wide variety of electronic resources that can be useful for the classroom. Among the most popular have been CD-ROM document collections such as *Chaucer: Life & Times; Pennsylvania Gazette, 1728–1783;* and *Presidential Papers: Washington-Clinton.* Textbook publishers are increasingly providing electronic study guides, map exercises, sample presentation slides, and computerized test banks on CD-ROM, floppy disks, or even on the Web. Some schools are producing, or arranging access to, large collections of digital materials.

The most extensive, if still not fully developed, source for electronic resources is the World Wide Web. Many web sites can deliver primary documents, secondary literature, sound, and images from a wide variety of sources. Students who explore web sites related to a course can bring compelling evidence and arguments back to the class. Publishers are building companion web sites around their textbooks, and large international projects have been launched to provide on-line sources for standard humanities and social science survey courses. Finally, libraries and scholars are making scanned materials accessible over the Web, although the copyright implications of this practice require close attention.

In all these cases, the relatively new forms of material require some special handling. You should approach selecting electronic sources for your course with the following guidelines in mind:

- Ensure that all electronic assignments contribute to the objectives of the course. The new materials should pass the same relevance test as traditional material.
- Personally evaluate the scholarly quality of your electronic sources. Although linking to electronic sources might be free, one substandard source can lower the credibility of the course.
- Use the appropriate medium. Can these materials be more easily or effectively used in a more

traditional form? Try to use the Web for things that it can do particularly well: displaying multimedia material, hyperlinking to other sources, providing interactive experiences, or improving access to otherwise cumbersome or distant materials. As on-line archives begin providing access to recordings and radio and television programs, its possible value to teachers will increase even further.

- When dealing with massive collections of primary documents, make the task of using them more manageable by discussing ahead of time the particular questions the collection might help answer. Then divide the class into groups, each of which will explore the archive with a particular question in mind. Short review papers, webpage postings, or in-class presentations can enable each group to share small numbers of documents, images, and other artifacts that address the question or theme they have chosen.

- Reinforce traditional research skills. Using on-line information requires at least as much skill and discipline as using traditional sources. Just because students can "cut and paste" from on-line sources, the process of researching and writing is not fundamentally different from that for a project that uses more traditional sources. Encourage students to take the same detailed notes and to follow the same strict citation procedures they use for conventional printed sources.

- Mix traditional and electronic sources. Require students to consult traditional printed and microform source material as well as electronic resources. Most valuable sources will not be digitized any time soon, if ever, so student research should include at least as many traditional sources as electronic ones. Students wedded to the Internet sometimes tend to assume that they need never use a traditional library; some act at times as if they think information that is not on the Web does not exist. Be sure that you structure assignments in a way that does not sever your students' ties to the most important sources of scholarly material.

- Caution your students to be especially critical readers of on-line sources. Explain the Web's fluid (or nonexistent) editorial standards and the need to determine the standards, origin, and scholarly discipline that went into the creation of each on-line source. Virtually anyone can create a web site, and there is no review process to test sites for accuracy or reliability unless the creator of the site initiates one. To avoid the problems such lax standards can cause, you should heavily emphasize the on-line offerings of established libraries, archives, and universities.

- To ensure that your students become critical consumers of on-line material, consider having them complete a quick questionnaire after reading the first electronic resource of the term. Ask them to identify the author of the material, give the address (URL) for the site, and comment on the scholarly methods and reputation of the sponsoring organization or individual. Have them try to discover how long a site has been in existence and how long the reference will remain on-line. Will more material be added or corrections made? How should they cite this material in their papers, and can they be sure the material will still be at that location? A short discussion of the answers in class will counteract many of the sources of confusion and disappointment.

ELECTRONIC PUBLISHING OF
STUDENT WORK

Ordinarily, when students write essays or research papers for a course, they write for an audience of one: the instructor. But teachers who have persuaded students that they are writing for a broader audience have found that students take the work more seriously and devote a great deal more effort to it. Creating a system of on-line publications for your course, or for your department, can have a tremendous impact on student engagement with scholarly work. On-line publishing also creates opportunities for student collaboration, and for students to take a more direct and responsible role in the learning process than they otherwise might. Another thing that makes electronic publishing valuable is that it exposes students to the stylistic constraints and opportunities of the new digital media. Already, a considerable portion of this nation's business, scholarly, and personal communication occurs through e-mail, the World Wide Web, and private networks of computers. A number of important periodicals, such as *Salon Magazine* and Microsoft's *Slate,* exist primarily or solely on-line.

The range of electronic publishing techniques you use in your course depends largely on the technical skills, resources, and imagination of you or your class. Students have performed the following with considerable success:

- *Multimedia in-class presentations:* A student uses a presentation program to supplement a standard spoken presentation with images, charts and graphs, or sound.
- *Essays in the form of World Wide Web pages:* While even a traditional text essay might be posted for comment, the best web essays will make use of the Web's unique ability to incorporate multimedia elements.
- *Web teaching units for your class or other*

classes: Students can become teachers by sharing their research and analysis with the class or with an outside audience (including secondary and primary school classes).

- *Web exhibits:* By emulating the form and rigor of museum and library exhibits, students can produce a classroom and community resource on their topic.
- *Collaborative projects:* All of the above projects lend themselves to collaborative work by groups of students.
- *Classroom archive/library:* Over the years, a digitally savvy course might accumulate an excellent library of digital student essays, teaching units, exhibits, and dialogues.

The promise of electronic publishing is almost evenly matched by its perils. The following steps will help you avoid the most common pitfalls:

- Establish and communicate the pedagogical goals of the assignment. You should justify deviation from traditional forms of student work by establishing that the innovation will improve the students' knowledge, skills, or learning experience.
- Make the assignment appropriate to the medium. Most rewarding are assignments that make use of multimedia sources, hyperlinks, and collaboration with resources or people over the Internet. For text-only essays, ensure that the students' classmates or an outside scholar or peer comments on the published papers.
- Provide appropriate technical and stylistic support. Even if the assignment is voluntary, many students will need help with the new requirements of publishing on-line or preparing multimedia presentations. Arrange for help from your

school's computer department, devote a particular class to a group tutorial, or devote a portion of your office hours to technical assistance. Teaching computing skills in non–computer science classes is a controversial practice; be sure not to allow the technology to overwhelm the substance.

- Keep technological hurdles as low as possible. If possible, use web page templates, simple submission forms, and any other aid that can keep the focus of the class on the subject matter and not the tools. Keep abreast of the range of technical skill among your students through classroom and schoolwide surveys, or even a show of hands on the first day of class.

- Arrange campus, local, scholarly, or international exposure for your students' work. The publishing aspect of the Web is too often assumed to happen spontaneously. A moderate effort at planning how to distribute and publicize your students' work can ensure that students feel their publications have been taken seriously.

- Integrate and archive student work on the course home page. Many students appreciate contributing to the knowledge of the class and to the learning experience of their peers. A gallery of past student work is also effective advertising of your course to prospective students. Pay careful attention to privacy issues regarding student work; school policy and privacy laws may require pseudonyms and anonymous entries when student work is exposed to an outside audience. Certainly nothing should ever be published without the express permission of its author.

As promising as these new media forms might be, the lack of clear standards for evaluating this work has sometimes hampered their adoption. Teachers are comfortable guiding and evaluating students on traditional essays and presentations. Multimedia presentations or web pages require even more explicit guidelines to avoid highly uneven results. Electronic projects should fulfill the assignment, make appropriate use of multimedia material, conform to on-line style conventions, and respect the diversity and size of their potential audience.

MULTIMEDIA LECTURING

Despite several generations of harsh criticism, lecturing remains one of the most common, and often one of the most effective, means of teaching. At its best, a lecture enlivens academic subjects with the instructor's energy and curiosity and with the persuasive nuances of human speech. Nevertheless, lecturing has its limits, most notably the reputed twelve-minute average human attention span, the difficulty of representing complex material verbally, and the awkwardness of presenting diverse, multimedia sources.

These challenges have already led teachers to use chalkboards, overhead and slide projectors, and audiovisual equipment. Some schools are beginning to provide classrooms equipped with built-in or portable multimedia computer systems. You can take advantage of the electronic possibilities for lecturing by familiarizing yourself with the most popular and powerful computerized classroom tool: presentation software such as Microsoft PowerPoint. Business presenters were the early adopters of this software, driven by the less captive nature of their audiences. Teachers have recently begun to use such programs to consolidate into one device the presentation of multimedia material that supplements their lectures.

The basic concept behind presentation software is a familiar one; it is the same as that for the slide show or overhead transparencies. The most elementary use of presentation programs is as a glorified slide projector to display a sequence of pictures or documents to accompany your lecture. When using computerized presentation, however, you can easily add captions to the images, digitally highlight or annotate them, or combine multiple images on a single "slide." Teachers who distribute lecture outlines or write them on the board might want to include that text on a projected slide.

At their most advanced, these programs can allow teachers to add sound, video, and even interactive charts and graphs to slides. You might, for example, project a map that demonstrates various changes as you advance along a time line. If the classroom computer system has Internet access, you can hyperlink your slides to World Wide Web resources, effectively incorporating that material into your lecture.

The use of presentation software in the classroom requires careful planning and a not inconsiderable investment of time. You should be prepared to take some or all of the following steps:

- Determine whether you have access to the equipment and special classrooms necessary to display electronic presentations. At a minimum, you will need a laptop computer, a projection device compatible with your software and hardware, and a classroom with a convenient electrical outlet, dimmable lights, and an appropriate screen. Check that the computer is capable of producing all the effects you plan for the class such as sound, video, or Internet access.
- Ensure that your own computer equipment will allow you to create and maintain these presentations. Manipulating multimedia resources requires a relatively powerful computer and, with some exceptions, a modern graphical operating

system such as Microsoft Windows or the Macintosh Operating System.

- Acquire a presentation program. Many of the more popular office suites (for instance, from Microsoft, Corel, or Lotus) include them. Your campus may already have purchased licenses to one or more of these products. Finally, check to make sure your choice is compatible with the systems installed in classrooms.

- Write or revise your lectures with the multimedia slide show in mind. Begin to collect compelling pictures and artwork, explanatory maps and charts, music clips, even short videos that might enhance your analysis. Evaluate which of these materials can be rendered in digital form, and consider the copyright implications—if possible by discussing them with the relevant experts in your school. When preparing text for your presentation—headings or explanatory captions— use simple clauses and standard fonts (for example, Arial or Times New Roman) to ensure that your presentation will look the same regardless of what computer you are using. The best font size for headings is twenty-four point, although you can use thirty point or larger if you wish.

- Be sure to calculate how long a visual or audio presentation will take and how much of a reduction in the other parts of your lecture may be necessary.

- Digitize the material that best advances your teaching goals. Your campus may have a central lab for digitizing materials, and you might find some of the equipment affordable enough for a department or individual to own. Make the file size of the slides as small as possible, even if it means sacrificing a little of the display quality. These images and sounds will typically be experienced on a large screen or in a noisy room, so fine details might be lost in any case.

- Keep the design of your electronic slides simple and efficient. Include only material that directly supports the point you are making in the lecture. Eliminate all unnecessary special effects, backgrounds, and animation.

- Proofread and test your presentations thoroughly on your machine and in the classroom. Pay special attention to the legibility and overall quantity of text on your slides. And be sure your work is stored in at least two different places. Concentrating your multimedia material on one machine or one disk may be convenient, but this also creates a single point of failure in the notoriously fickle personal computer.

- Have a backup plan. Make sure that you will be able to deliver the main substance of your lecture whether or not everything works perfectly. In the case of equipment failure, do not waste class time trying to solve the problem.

- Plan to publish your slide shows on the course home page, if you have one. While traditional slide shows are difficult to reproduce for absent students or to review at exam time, many presentation programs offer a relatively simple procedure for publishing your show on the Web.

- Use electronic resources to help encourage student participation during your lectures—for example, by presenting a variety of images, primary documents, or other materials that could form the basis for an in-class debate or conversation.

ELECTRONIC DISCUSSIONS

Perhaps the most controversial (and probably the most common) application of technology is as a supplement to or replacement for face-to-face conversation. Small group discussions are an irreplaceable forum for teaching, learning, and thoughtful collaboration. They are not, however, without problems. Small discussion groups are an expensive way to organize teaching, and as a result they are becoming less common in some of the budget-conscious schools and universities of our time. Some students—shy people, or those who are not native English speakers—are uncomfortable in small group discussions and do not actively participate in them. Students speaking in a classroom setting can make superficial contributions that would have benefited from more advance preparation. On-line discussions can help compensate for these problems.

On-line discussion tools fall into two basic categories: synchronous (chat) and asynchronous (e-mail, mailing lists, and threaded discussions). In a synchronous discussion, students in effect talk to one another over the Internet in much the same way they speak on the telephone; in asynchronous discussions, the communication is more like an exchange of letters, even if potentially much more rapid. In general, classes with no face-to-face meetings are the best candidates for synchronous on-line discussions that approximate the dynamic and serendipitous qualities of small discussion groups. Classes that already meet together may prefer asynchronous electronic forums as a more useful supplement to their regular discussions. A class can also, of course, get the advantages of both by using an asynchronous discussion forum over the course of the term with periodic chat sessions for special guests or events.

The most basic, but still very useful, technique is to use the campus e-mail system to broadcast messages to your students. For large lecture courses or classes that require frequent out-of-class communication this method alone can save considerable amounts of time. E-mail lists—a group of e-mail addresses grouped under a single alias such as "english101" or "us-survey" and often known as a *listserve*—can be particularly useful for large classes. Lists can also allow members of the class to communicate with each other. Slightly more complicated and resource intensive are threaded discussion forums such as Usenet and various web-based forums; such forums keep a permanent record of each person's contribution so that each succeeding participant can review the entire course of a conversation and add his or her own contribution to it. Chat sessions take perhaps the most planning, the most specialized software, and considerable guidance on chat room etiquette and procedures.

To use electronic discussion tools in your class, consider the following steps:

- Determine whether electronic discussions contribute to your pedagogical goals. These tools require a significant time commitment from teacher and students and should only be used if they serve an important educational function. Most teachers turn to electronic discussions to get students thinking critically about the reading before they come to class, to answer questions of comprehension and fact as they occur, and to provide some continuity of thought between one week's topic and the next.
- Investigate the tools and practices of your campus. E-mail is the only technique that has near-universal support on campuses in the United States. Your ability to implement other forms of electronic discussions will be significantly shaped by your school's choice of additional communication tools.
- Make the on-line discussion substantive and

unique. Provide information in these sessions
that cannot be found elsewhere or at least not as
conveniently. On-line discussions can be a supplement to, or possibly a replacement for, some
of the communications that occur during office
hours. They can allow a student who has had a
conversation with you in your office to continue
that conversation with other questions and ideas
as they arise; and they can allow a student who
cannot attend your office hours or who was discouraged by a long line to communicate with
you in other ways.

- Think of particular purposes that would be well
  served by electronic discussions. You might, for
  example, create a web-based review session before an exam. Students can submit questions to
  you electronically, and you can respond to them
  by posting an answer on the Web that will be
  available to all the students in your class. You
  can organize similar targeted discussions at any
  point in a course.
- Consider the demands of on-line discussions in
  light of students' work load and time commitments. Balance any required participation with
  reduced demands in other areas of the course.
  Otherwise, you can expect students to be reluctant or resentful of the new tasks.
- Require or reward participation to prevent your
  on-line discussions from suffering the "empty
  restaurant syndrome" (the aura of failure that
  surrounds any place or project that attracts few
  visitors) or becoming the preserve of a small
  group of computer enthusiasts. Without clear
  guidance from the instructor about the importance of this activity, even many of your hardest-
  working students will decline to participate. One

particularly successful strategy is to assign one or two students in the class to post a discussion question at the beginning of each week, and another student or pair of students to write a response or follow-up message at the end of the week. Integrate on-line events (student presentations, debates, interaction with outside experts or other classes) into your course schedule.

- Evaluate the skills and habits of your students. Determine whether a simple list of e-mail addresses can meet your needs. Since many students already use e-mail for personal correspondence, e-mail messages about your course have a high chance of being read. Whatever system you use, you can dramatically reduce student confusion (and time-consuming requests for assistance) by distributing a detailed handout describing how students can perform such basic tasks as sending mail to your class list, reaching your course web site, or using a conferencing system.

- Republish (with permission from the authors and in edited form) interesting or provocative dialogues on the course web page or through handouts. Having their words taken seriously in this manner will encourage student participation.

- Evaluate accessibility problems. Off-campus, technologically challenged, and physically handicapped students may require special arrangements. Find out what campus resources are available to assist these groups.

Finally, to make these technologies work in your classroom, you must make regular contributions to the electronic discussions just as you would to a face-to-face discussion. On-line discussions have to be closely monitored to ensure their intellectual usefulness and to reinforce the importance of etiquette in this relatively unfamiliar terrain. You yourself must be a participant to ensure that students take them seriously. But guard your time. Be careful not to create an online discussion in which every query is directed at you. Your participation is essential, but you should not allow yourself to be overwhelmed with electronic communications.

Computer technology is becoming both more useful and more cost effective for many fields of teaching. And yet only you, the teacher, can determine whether these methods will prove effective in your classroom. Whatever you decide, remember that technology complements, but does not fundamentally alter, the elements of teaching.

AFTERWORD

WHY DO WE TEACH?

This book has attempted to answer a number of questions about how to teach, on the assumption that its readers are people with enough commitment to the academic life to want to teach well. But almost all teachers ask themselves at some point—even at many points—the question not of how to teach, but why. That is a question every teacher must answer, in some measure, alone. But we offer a few observations, drawn from our own experiences, on this central issue of academic life.

One of the realities of teaching, of course, is that the people who benefit most from what we do—our students—disappear from our lives quickly and usually permanently the moment they graduate (if not before) and give us few opportunities to see how we have affected them. And yet nothing is clearer from the long history of education than that good teachers—like good parents—play an enormously important role in the lives of many of their students; that they do, in fact, change students' lives. One of the rewards of good teaching, therefore, should be the knowledge that we have helped shape the futures of many people, that we have instilled modes of thinking, created intellectual passions, promoted forms of tolerance and understanding, and, of course, increased knowledge. That the beneficiaries of our efforts are often invisible to us in no way reduces the value of what we do.

Teaching has rewards to teachers themselves as well. The community of education and scholarship can be a lonely place at times, and can seem isolated from the larger world. But the academic life at its best is also a broadening life—a life of constant surprises and continuing intellectual growth; a life that forever expands our knowledge of the world and hence the richness of our experience in living out our lives; a life that gives us the opportunity to convey our own passion for what we know to others in the hope that some of them, at least, will come to share it. The wonder and excitement that we sometimes encounter in our students when we help them discover a new area of knowledge is rewarding to us, in part, because it helps us recapture that same wonder and excitement, which is continually within our grasp if we do not lose the will to find it.

Good teaching, finally, is valuable to society—in ways both obvious and obscure. Everyone agrees that education is important, and that effective teaching is the key to education. Students need many skills and much knowledge to succeed in today's rapidly changing world; there is a direct correlation between a person's level of education and his or her chances of professional and economic success in life. But education has another, less immediately visible, social value. It is a vehicle for creating knowledgeable, aware citizens who are capable of looking critically at the world in which they live and making informed decisions about their lives and the lives of others. Education is a way of keeping alive the true basis of democracy: the ability of people to know enough and understand enough about the great issues of their time to help guide their society into its future. In the discouraging moments that all teachers encounter from time to time, it is worth remembering this great goal—which, when things go well, also becomes the great achievement—of devoting one's life to education.

SUGGESTIONS FOR FURTHER READING

GENERAL WORKS

Baicco, Sharon A., and Jamie N. Dewaters. *Successful College Teaching: Problem-Solving Strategies of Distinguished Professors.* Boston: Allyn & Bacon, 1998.

Banner, James M., Jr., and Harold C. Cannon. *The Elements of Teaching.* New Haven, CT: Yale University Press, 1997.

Campbell, William E., and Karl A. Smith, eds. *New Paradigms for College Teaching.* Edina, MN: Interaction Book Company, 1997.

Chickering, Arthur W., and Selda Gamson, eds. *Applying the Seven Principles for Good Practice in Undergraduate Education.* San Francisco, CA: Jossey-Bass, 1991.

Committee on Undergraduate Science Education. *Science Teaching Reconsidered: A Handbook.* Washington, DC: National Academy Press, 1997.

Davidson, Cliff I., and Susan A. Ambrose. *The New Professor's Handbook: A Guide to Teaching and Research in Engineering and Science.* Bolton, MA: Anker Publishing Co. Inc., 1994.

Davis, Barbara Gross. *Tools for Teaching.* San Francisco, CA: Jossey-Bass, 1993.

Eble, Kenneth E. *The Craft of Teaching: A Guide to Mastering the Professor's Art.* San Francisco, CA: Jossey-Bass, 1988.

Fenstermacher, Gary D., and Jonas F. Soltis. *Approaches to Teaching.* New York: Teachers College Press, 1992.

Fried, Robert L., and Deborah Meier. *The Passionate Teacher.* Boston: Beacon Press, 1996.

Fuhrmann, Barbara Schneider, and Anthony F. Grasha. *A Practical*

Handbook for College Teachers. Boston: Little, Brown and Company, 1983.

Gibson, Gerald W. *Good Start: A Guidebook for New Faculty in Liberal Arts Colleges.* Bolton, MA: Anker Publishing Co. Inc., 1992.

Gullette, Margaret Morganroth, ed. *The Art and Craft of Teaching.* Cambridge, MA: Harvard University Press, 1984.

Highet, Gilbert. *The Art of Teaching.* New York: Vintage Books, 1989.

Hodge, Bonnie M., and Jennie Preston-Sabin, eds. *Accommodations— Or Just Good Teaching? Strategies for Teaching College Students with Disabilities.* Westport, CT: Praeger, 1997.

Lowman, Joseph. *Mastering the Techniques of Teaching.* San Francisco, CA: Jossey-Bass, 1984.

McKeachie, Wilbert J. *McKeachie's Teaching Tips: Strategies, Research, and Theory for College and University Teachers.* 10th ed. Boston: Houghton Mifflin Co., 1999.

Sawyer, R. McLaran, et al., eds. *The Art and Politics of College Teaching: A Practical Guide for the Beginning Professor.* New York: Peter Lang Publishing, Inc., 1992.

Stocking, S. Holly, et al. *More Quick Hits: Successful Strategies by Award-Winning Teachers.* Bloomington: Indiana University Press, 1998.

Weimer, Maryellen, and Rose Ann Neff, eds. *Teaching College: Collected Readings for the New Instructor.* Madison, WI: Atwood Publishing, 1998.

1 GETTING READY

"Effective Course Materials," "Selecting a Textbook," "Course Materials Review." *Teaching Professor* 1, no. 6 (August 1987): 1–4.

Mager, Robert F. *Preparing Instructional Objectives.* 2d ed. Belmont, CA: Fearon Publishers, Inc., 1975.

"One Syllabus That Encourages Thinking Not Just Learning." *Teaching Professor* 1, no. 6 (August 1987): 5.

Rubin, Sharon. "Professors, Students, and the Syllabus." *Chronicle of Higher Education* 7 (August 1985): 56.

2 THE FIRST WEEKS

Dorn, Dean S. "The First Day of Class: Problems and Strategies." *Teaching Sociology* 15, no. 1 (January 1987): 61–72.

"The First Day of Class: Advice and Ideas." *Teaching Professor* 3, no. 7 (1989): 1–2.

Fraher, Richard. "Learning a New Art: Suggestions for Beginning Teachers." Chap. 9 in *The Art and Craft of Teaching,* edited by Margaret Morganroth Gullette. Cambridge, MA: Harvard University Press, 1984.

Nash, Laura L. "The Rhythms of the Semester." Chap. 6 in *The Art and Craft of Teaching*, ed. Margaret Morganroth Gullette. Cambridge, MA: Harvard University Press, 1984.

"What to Do on the First Day of Class (The Round Table)." *English Journal* 77, no. 5 (September 1988): 89–91.

3 CLASSROOM DISCUSSIONS

Bowers, C. A., and David J. Flinders. *Responsive Teaching: An Ecological Approach to Classroom Patterns of Language, Culture, and Thought.* New York: Teachers College Press, 1990.

Brockbank, Anne, and Ian McGill. *Facilitating Reflective Learning in Higher Education.* Philadelphia: Society for Research into Higher Education and Open University Press, 1998.

Edwards, Clifford H. *Classroom Discipline and Management.* Upper Saddle River, NJ: Prentice Hall, 1996.

Emmer, Edmund T., et al. *Classroom Management for Secondary Teachers.* Boston: Allyn & Bacon, 1997.

Frederick, Peter. "The Dreaded Discussion: Ten Ways to Start." *Improving College and University Teaching* 29, no. 3 (summer 1981): 109–14.

Hill, William Fawcett. *William Fawcett Hill's Learning through Discussion.* 3d ed. Thousand Oaks, CA: Sage Publications, 1994.

4 THE ART AND CRAFT OF LECTURING

Alexander, James D. "Lectures: The Ethics of Borrowing." *College Teaching* 36, no. 1 (winter 1988): 20–24.

Blackey, Robert. "New Wine in Old Bottles: Revitalizing the Traditional History Lecture." *Teaching History* 22, no. 1 (spring 1997): 3–25.

Frederick, Peter J. "The Lively Lecture—Eight Variations." *College Teaching* 34, no. 2 (spring 1986): 43–50.

Geske, J. "Overcoming the Drawbacks of the Large Lecture Class." *College Teaching* 40, no. 4 (1992): 151–54.

Gullette, Margaret Morganroth. "Leading Discussion in a Lecture Course: Some Maxims and an Exhortation." *Change* 24, no. 2 (March/April 1992): 32–39.

Penner, Jon G. *Why Many College Teachers Cannot Lecture: How to Avoid Communication Breakdown in the Classroom.* Springfield, IL: Charles C. Thomas, 1984.

Sitler, Helen Collins. "The Spaced Lecture." *College Teaching* 45, no. 3 (summer 1997): 108–10.

Weimer, Maryellen Gleason, ed. *Teaching Large Classes Well.* New Directions for Teaching and Learning, no. 32. San Francisco, CA: Jossey-Bass, winter 1992.

5 STUDENT WRITING AND RESEARCH

"Make the Most of Written Feedback." *Teaching Professor* 5, no. 7 (1991): 1–2.

Malehorn, H. "Term Papers for Sale and What to Do about It." *Improving College and University Teaching* 31, no. 3 (1983): 107–8.

Simon, L. "The Papers We Want to Read." *College Teaching* 36, no. 1 (1988): 6–8.

Walvoord, B. F. *Helping Students Write Well: A Guide for Teachers in All Disciplines.* 2d ed. New York: Modern Language Association, 1986.

6 TESTING AND EVALUATION

Angelo, Thomas A., and Kathryn P. Cross. *Classroom Assessment Techniques: A Handbook for College Teachers.* 2d ed. San Francisco, CA: Jossey-Bass, 1993.

Blackey, Robert, ed. *History Anew: Innovations in the Teaching of History Today.* Long Beach, CA: University Press of California State University, 1993.

"Exams: Alternative Ideas and Approaches." *Teaching Professor* 3, no. 8 (1990): 3–4.

Jacobs, L. C., and C. I. Chase. *Developing and Using Tests Effectively: A Guide for Faculty.* San Francisco, CA: Jossey-Bass, 1992.

Murray, John P. "Better Testing for Better Learning." *College Teaching* 38, no. 4 (fall 1990): 148–52.

7 EVALUATING YOUR TEACHING

Doyle, Kenneth O. *Student Evaluation of Instruction.* Lexington, MA: Lexington Books (D. C. Heath), 1975.

Eble, Kenneth E. *The Recognition and Evaluation of Teaching.* Salt Lake City: Project to Improve College Teaching, 1970.

England, James, Pat Hutchings, and Wilbert J. McKeachie. *The Professional Evaluation of Teaching.* New York: American Council of Learned Societies, 1996.

Krupnick, Catherine G. "The Uses of Videotape Replay." In *Teaching and the Case Method: Text, Cases, and Readings,* edited by C. Roland Christensen with Abby J. Hansen, 256–63. Boston: Harvard Business School, 1987.

"Teaching Journals: A Self-Evaluation Strategy." *Teaching Professor* 2, no. 6 (June 1988): 2.

Weimer, Maryellen. *Improving College Teaching: Strategies for Developing Instructional Effectiveness.* San Francisco, CA: Jossey-Bass, 1990.

8 TEACHING AS A GRADUATE STUDENT

Bernstein, Harvey R. *Manual for Teaching Assistants*. Ithaca, NY: Cornell University, Center for Improvement of Undergraduate Education, 1975.

Edgerton, Russell, Patricia Hutchings, and Kathleen Quinlan. *The Teaching Portfolio: Capturing the Scholarship in Teaching*. Washington, DC: American Association for Higher Education, 1991.

Keith-Spiegal, Patricia, et al. *The Ethics of Teaching: A Casebook*. Muncie, IN: Ball State University, 1993.

Lambert, Leo, Stacey Lane Tice, and Patricia H. Featherstone, eds. *University Teaching: A Guide for Graduate Students*. Syracuse, NY: Syracuse University Press, 1996.

Nyquist, Jody, et al., eds. *Preparing the Professoriate of Tomorrow to Teach: Selected Readings in TA Training*. Dubuque, IA: Kendall Hunt Publishing Co., 1991.

Schneider, Beth E. "Graduate Women, Sexual Harassment, and University Policy." *Journal of Higher Education* 58, no. 1 (January/ February 1987): 46–65.

Segerstrale, Ullica. "The Multifaceted Role of the Section Leader." Chap. 5 in *The Art and Craft of Teaching*, edited by Margaret Morganroth Gullette. Cambridge, MA: Harvard University Press, 1984.

9 TEACHING INCLUSIVELY IN A MULTICULTURAL AGE

Allison, Clinton B. *Present and Past: Essays for Teachers in the History of Education*. New York: Peter Lang Publishing, Inc., 1995.

Border, Laura L. B., and Nancy Van Note Chism. *Teaching for Diversity*. New Directions for Teaching and Learning, no. 49. San Francisco, CA: Jossey-Bass, spring 1992.

Ladson-Billings, Gloria. *The Dream Keepers: Successful Teachers of African American Children*. San Francisco, CA: Jossey-Bass, 1994.

Spring, Joel H. *Deculturalization and the Struggle for Equality: A Brief History of the Education of Dominated Cultures in the United States*. 2d ed. New York: McGraw-Hill, 1997.

10 USING ELECTRONIC RESOURCES FOR TEACHING

Albright, Michal J., and David L. Graf, eds. *Teaching in the Information Age: The Role of Educational Technology*. New Directions for Teaching and Learning, no 51. San Francisco, CA: Jossey-Bass, 1992.

Chickering, Arthur W., and Stephen Ehrmann. "Implementing the

Seven Principles: Technology as a Lever." *American Association for Higher Education Bulletin* (October 1996).

Kozma, R. B., and J. Johnston. "The Technological Revolution Comes to the Classroom." *Change* 23, no. 1 (1991): 10–23.

Laurillard, Diana. *Rethinking University Teaching: A Framework for the Effective Use of Educational Technology.* New York: Routledge, 1993.

Poole, Bernard John. *Education for an Information Age: Teaching in the Computerized Classroom.* 2d ed. Boston: WCB/McGraw-Hill, 1997.

Truman, Myron C., ed. *Literacy Online: The Promise (and Peril) of Reading and Writing with Computers.* Pittsburgh, PA: Pittsburgh University Press, 1992.

ABOUT THE AUTHORS

Alan Brinkley is the Allan Nevins Professor of History at Columbia University. He taught previously at MIT, Harvard (where he was awarded the Joseph R. Levenson Memorial Teaching Prize), and the City University of New York Graduate School. Among his publications are *Voices of Protest: Huey Long, Father Coughlin, and the Great Depression* (which won the National Book Award); *The End of Reform: New Deal Liberalism in Recession and War; Liberalism and its Discontents;* and two college textbooks, *American History: A Survey* and *The Unfinished Nation: A Concise History of the American People.*

Betty Abrahamsen Dessants is assistant professor of history at Florida State University. She is a historian of American foreign relations, and her current work analyzes the relationship between the federal government and American scholars in developing strategic intelligence on the Soviet Union during World War II and the Cold War. Her work has appeared in the journal *Intelligence and National Security.* Prior to teaching at the university level, she taught history in secondary public and independent schools. She has given numerous presentations on the craft of teaching.

Michael W. Flamm is assistant professor of history at Ohio Wesleyan University. He taught previously at public high schools in New Jersey and New York. He is the author of several articles that have appeared in scholarly journals, and of the forthcoming *"Law and Order": Street Crime, Civil Disorder, and the Crisis of Liberalism.*

Cynthia Griggs Fleming is associate professor of cultural studies, history, and African-American studies at the University of Tennessee, Knoxville. She is the author of *Soon We Will Not Cry: The Liberation of Ruby Doris Smith Robinson,* and of numerous articles in scholarly journals.

Charles Forcey, Jr., is a Ph.D. candidate in modern American intellectual history at Columbia University. He has been an instructor at Columbia and is presently vice president for new media at Clio Inc., Visualizing History, where his projects have included interactive maps, web sites, and CD-ROMs for classroom use. He makes frequent presentations on electronic teaching and research methods.

Eric Rothschild is a history teacher who retired in 1998 as chair of the Social Studies Department at Scarsdale High School after thirty-six years in the classroom. He has also taught at Manhattan College and LaSalle University. He was New York State Social Studies Educator of the Year in 1991 and served on the executive board of the Organization of American History from 1991 to 1994. He has written extensively on advanced placement and on simulations and is the author of *The New York Times School Microfilm Collection.*

INDEX

academic honesty, 15, 123

activities, classroom, 19–21, 86, 105, 111

Adventures of Huckleberry Finn, The, 141

Amazon.com, 8

anonymity, in evaluations, 103

anxiety, at beginning of course, 17, 59

assignments, 29–30, 103, 106–7, 113, 124, 130, 143, 149, 157, 159; assembling teaching units on-line, 145; essay, 3, 156, 159; exhibit building on-line, 145, 157; independent projects, 65–66, 68, 85, 103, 137; papers, 3–4, 13–15, 29–30, 37, 46–48, 54, 85, 119, 124, 143, 145, 150, 154, 156; papers, primary source, 69–70, 75; in preparation for discussion, 37–38, 44–45; reading, 1, 6, 10–15, 29, 36–38, 54, 69, 71, 87, 93, 102–3, 105–6, 123, 143, 145, 150, 164;

reading, on-line, 144, 150–52; research, 65, 68, 73, 82, 112, 117; research, on-line, 153–55; writing, 37–38, 65–84, 85, 95; writing, format of, 74; writing, length of, 73

attendance, 14

audio recordings, 5–6, 10, 95, 150, 153–54

Barnes and Noble, web-based service, 8

behavior, in class, 123–24

bias, 136, 141

Birth of a Nation, The, 140–41

blackboard, use of, 7, 38, 40–41, 59–60, 159

blue books, 96

book exhibits, 9

books, as course materials, 6, 8–11, 15, 130

Books in Print, 9

bookstores, 8–10; campus, 9–10

Bowker's Complete Video Directory, 10